Profitable Properties

The Art of Real Estate Investing

Cheryl Waller, MBA

ISBN: 9798396385900

TABLE OF CONTENTS

THE LURE OF REAL ESTATE INVESTING: AN INTRODUCTION

Welcome to the beginning of your journey into the world of real estate investing, an adventure teeming with potential rewards and robust opportunities. This inaugural chapter, is designed to set the stage, providing you with a broad perspective on why real estate continues to attract investors from all walks of life.

In the realm of investing, real estate has a unique appeal. Its tangible nature, the ability to touch and see your investments, is only one aspect of its allure. The opportunities for building wealth through capital appreciation, the potential for creating a stream of passive income, and the various tax advantages available make real estate an investment avenue of choice for many.

However, as attractive as these benefits may be, it's also vital to acknowledge the complexities inherent in real estate investing. This field isn't just about buying property and watching your wealth grow; it involves a range of strategies, financial commitments, understanding market dynamics, and careful management. It's essential to approach real estate investing with an open mind, ready to learn and adapt.

This book provides an overview of the many facets of real estate investing, seeking to uncover its enticing nature. Whether you're an aspiring investor eager to explore the possibilities, or a seasoned investor looking to expand your knowledge, this book sets the foundation for your understanding.

As we navigate through the intricacies and nuances of real estate investing, this book aims to serve as your comprehensive guide. It is designed to help you make informed, strategic decisions that align with your financial goals.

So, let's embark on this journey together, exploring the captivating world of real estate, and unravel the secrets behind its enduring appeal.

DECODING REAL ESTATE: KEY TERMS AND CONCEPTS

Welcome to the next stage of your real estate investing journey – understanding the language of real estate. This chapter, "Decoding Real Estate: Key Terms and Concepts," is designed to familiarize you with the essential jargon, concepts, and terminologies that form the backbone of any real estate conversation.

Much like any specialized field, real estate has its unique lingo, a collection of terms that can seem like a foreign language to the uninitiated. From 'amortization' to 'zoning', the language of real estate can often be intricate and nuanced. However, grasping these terms is crucial to understand the complexities of the industry and to converse effectively with other professionals in the field.

But fear not, this chapter is here to demystify these complex terms and make them accessible. We will delve into essential concepts like property types, appraisal, equity, mortgage, capital gains, depreciation, and so much more. Each term will be explained in easy-to-understand language, with real-life examples wherever possible to provide context and clarity.

By the end of this chapter, you'll be able to speak the language of real estate with confidence. You'll be able to understand the discussions, contracts, and reports that are a vital part of any real estate investment. You'll also be better equipped to make informed decisions, as you'll understand the implications of these key terms and concepts on your investment strategy.

So, let's embark on this journey of decoding the language of real estate. Remember, understanding is the first step to mastery, and mastering the language of real estate is a crucial step towards successful investing.

Key Terms and Concepts

Understanding key terms and concepts is vital to mastering real estate investing. Here are some foundational terms:

- Real Estate: Real estate refers to physical property. This includes land and any buildings or structures on it, including homes, commercial buildings, and industrial properties. It can also encompass natural resources attached to the land.

- Investment Property: This is a real estate property purchased with the intention of earning a return on the investment, either through rental income, property value appreciation, or both.

- Appraisal: An appraisal is a professional's estimation of a property's value. Appraisals are conducted by licensed appraisers and consider factors like the property's condition, location, and comparison with similar properties recently sold in the area.

- Equity: Equity refers to the difference between a property's market value and the outstanding amount of the loans secured by the property. As you pay down the loan or the property's value increases, your equity grows.

- Mortgage: This is a loan taken out to buy property or land. The property or land serves as collateral for the loan.

- Capital Gains: This is the profit made from selling a property for more than you paid for it. Depending on how long you owned the property, these gains may be subject to taxes.

- Depreciation: This refers to the loss in value of a property over time due to wear and tear, aging, and other factors. For investment properties, depreciation can provide significant tax advantages.

- Cash Flow: In real estate investing, cash flow is the net income generated from an investment property after deducting all expenses, including mortgage payments, maintenance costs, property taxes, and insurance.

- Real Estate Investment Trust (REIT): A REIT is a company that owns, operates, or finances income-generating real estate. Investors can buy shares in a REIT, providing an avenue for real estate investment without the need to own property directly.

These terms form the backbone of real estate investing. Understanding them is the first step towards making informed investment decisions in the real estate market.

PROPERTY TYPES: RESIDENTIAL, COMMERCIAL, AND BEYOND

Welcome to the next leg of your journey into real estate investing. In this chapter, we turn our focus towards understanding the different types of properties you can invest in.

The real estate sector is diverse, encompassing a wide range of property types, each with its unique characteristics, investment potential, and associated risks. Some investors may be drawn towards the familiarity of residential properties, while others may see greater opportunities in commercial or industrial real estate. Still, others might find their niche in specialized real estate sectors such as agricultural lands or real estate investment trusts (REITs).

This chapter aims to guide you through this varied landscape. We will delve into the main categories of real estate: residential, commercial, industrial, and other specialized sectors. For each category, we will discuss their sub-types, investment considerations, potential returns, and risks involved. We'll also touch on the factors that influence the value and rentability of each property type, from location and size to market trends and zoning laws.

As we progress through this chapter, you will gain the knowledge needed to identify the type of real estate that aligns best with your investment goals, risk tolerance, and resources. By the end, you should feel confident in your ability to choose the right property type for your investment portfolio.

So, let's take a closer look at the diverse world of real estate property types, where every building, every parcel of land, represents a unique investment opportunity.

Residential Real Estate

Residential real estate includes properties that serve as a dwelling for individuals, families, or small groups. The primary purpose is non-business. This category has several sub-types, each with its unique investment considerations, potential returns, and risks.

Sub-Types
- -

- Single-Family Homes: These are standalone houses meant for one family or individual. They come in various architectural styles and sizes.

- Multi-Family Homes: These are buildings designed to house more than one family. Examples include duplexes, triplexes, and quadplexes.

- Apartments/Condominiums: These are buildings divided into individual units owned separately. The common areas are jointly owned by all unit owners.

- Townhouses: These are individually owned houses that share one or more walls with other similarly styled houses in a community.

- Mobile Homes: These are prefabricated homes built in factories and then transported to the site where they will be occupied.

Investment Considerations

- Location: The value of residential real estate is greatly influenced by its location. Proximity to good schools, amenities, transportation, and the safety of the neighborhood are vital factors.

- Property Condition: The state of the property affects its value and the rental income it can generate. A property in good condition will attract better rents and have fewer vacancies.

- Market Trends: Understanding the supply and demand in the local housing market can guide investment decisions.

Potential Returns

- Rental Income: The most direct form of return from residential real estate is the income generated from renting out the property.

- Appreciation: Over time, properties usually appreciate in value, and this can be realized when the property is sold.

Risks Involved

- Vacancies: If a property remains vacant for a long period, the lost rental income can be a significant financial drain.

- Bad Tenants: Dealing with irresponsible tenants who may damage the property or fail to pay rent on time can be a challenging aspect of residential real estate investing.

- Market Risks: Residential property values can fluctuate due to changes in the economy, interest rates, and local market conditions.

- Maintenance and Repair Costs: Unexpected repairs or regular maintenance can significantly impact the profitability of a property.

Understanding these factors can help guide your investment decisions in residential real estate and lead to a successful and profitable venture.

Commercial Real Estate

Commercial real estate is property that is used for business purposes. The primary goal of owning commercial real estate is to generate profit, either from rental income or capital gain. This category includes a variety of sub-types, each offering unique investment opportunities, potential returns, and risks.

Sub-Types

- Office Buildings: These range from small professional buildings to large skyscrapers and can be subdivided into Class A, B, and C based on construction quality, location, and amenities.

- Retail Properties: These include shopping centers, strip malls, and standalone stores. Retail properties often involve more complex leases, including terms like percentage rents.

- Industrial Properties: This category includes warehouses, factories, and distribution centers. These properties can be simpler to manage but might require specialized facilities.

- Multi-family Properties: This refers to residential properties with five or more units, such as apartment buildings or high-rise residential buildings.

- Hotel/Resort Properties: These are businesses that provide paid lodging, usually on a short-term basis. They can vary in size and type, from boutique hotels to luxury resorts.

Investment Considerations

- Location: The location is crucial in commercial real estate. Accessibility, visibility, and proximity to suppliers, customers, or workers can affect a property's attractiveness to tenants.

- Lease Agreements: Lease terms and tenant quality are critical. Longer-term leases can provide stable income, but might require concessions from the landlord.

- Market Trends: Understanding supply and demand dynamics in the area, along with broader economic factors, is important for making sound investment decisions.

Potential Returns

- Rental Income: The primary source of income from commercial properties is the rent paid by tenants. Commercial leases often last multiple years, providing more predictable income than residential properties.

- Appreciation: Commercial properties can also appreciate in value over time, providing capital gains upon sale.

- Tax Benefits: Depreciation and interest deductions can provide significant tax benefits for commercial property owners.

Risks Involved

- Economic Volatility: Commercial real estate can be significantly impacted by economic downturns. In hard times, businesses may fail, leading to high vacancy rates.

- Property Management: Commercial properties often require more complex management, including maintenance, lease negotiation, and dealing with business tenants' needs.

- Large Capital Requirements: Commercial properties generally have higher purchase prices and maintenance costs than residential properties, which can lead to higher financial risk.

Understanding these elements will help you navigate the commercial real estate market, balancing the potential returns against the inherent risks.

Industrial Real Estate

Industrial real estate is a property category focused on spaces used for manufacturing, production, storage, and distribution of goods. Given its unique characteristics, industrial real estate offers different investment considerations, potential returns, and risks compared to residential or commercial real estate.

Sub-Types

- Warehouses: These are large buildings usually situated near transport hubs. They are used for storing goods before they're distributed to various locations.

- Manufacturing Facilities: These properties are designed for the production of goods. They often require significant infrastructure for their operations, such as high-capacity electricity supply or waste disposal systems.

- Flex Industrial: These properties combine uses like office space, warehouse, and light manufacturing into one facility. They provide flexibility for businesses with diverse needs.

- Data Centers: As the digital economy grows, so does the demand for data storage, leading to a rise in data center real estate.

- Cold Storage: These are refrigerated warehouses used for storing perishable goods.

Investment Considerations

- Location: Proximity to transportation hubs (ports, highways, airports) is crucial for reducing logistics costs.

- Building Specifications: The utility of industrial buildings heavily depends on their specifications - ceiling heights, floor load, truck courts, etc.

- Market Demand: Understanding the local and global economic trends affecting the industrial sector is key.

Potential Returns

- Rental Income: Industrial properties can provide steady income, often with longer lease terms compared to residential properties.

- Capital Appreciation: Over time, industrial properties can appreciate in value, particularly in areas with growing demand.

Risks Involved

- Economic Factors: Changes in the economy can significantly impact industrial property demand.

- Obsolescence: Technological advances or changes in industry practices can make certain property features obsolete.

- Environmental Issues: Industrial properties can be subject to environmental regulations and potential contamination issues, which may require costly remediation.

Understanding the unique factors at play in industrial real estate can help investors effectively evaluate opportunities in this sector.

Other Specialized Sectors in Real Estate

Beyond the more common categories, there are numerous specialized sectors in real estate that cater to unique market needs. These can present interesting opportunities for investors, though they often require a deeper understanding of the specific sector.

Sub-Types

- Hospitality Properties: This category includes hotels, motels, bed-and-breakfast establishments, and short-term vacation rentals. They cater to travelers and tourists and are heavily dependent on the health of the travel and tourism industry.

- Healthcare Real Estate: This sector includes hospitals, medical offices, senior housing, and long-term care facilities. It is closely tied to trends in healthcare delivery and demographics.

- Student Housing: These are properties located near colleges and universities and designed specifically to cater to students.

- Self-storage: These facilities provide personal storage space for individuals and businesses. They're often used during transitions such as moving, downsizing, or business expansion.

- Agricultural Land: This includes farmland and ranchland. Its value is tied to agricultural commodity prices and sometimes to development potential.

Investment Considerations

- Specialized Knowledge: These sectors often require a deep understanding of the industry they serve. Regulations, consumer trends, and industry-specific risks can heavily impact success.

- Management Intensity: Some specialized sectors, like hospitality or healthcare, can be management-intensive, requiring high levels of service and regulatory compliance.

Potential Returns

- Rental Income: Some specialized properties, like student housing or self-storage, generate income through rents.

- Operating Income: For sectors like hospitality, income comes from business operations – e.g., room fees, food and beverage sales.

Risks Involved

- Sector-Specific Risks: These can range from travel industry fluctuations affecting hospitality properties to changes in government healthcare reimbursement impacting senior housing.

- Regulatory Risk: Some sectors, particularly healthcare, are heavily regulated, and changes in laws or regulations can impact profitability.

- Higher Capital Expenditure: Due to their specialized nature, these properties may require more significant capital expenditure to remain competitive.

Investing in these specialized sectors can provide unique opportunities and diversification. However, success often requires an understanding of the specific sector's dynamics and a readiness to manage the associated risks.

INVESTMENT STRATEGIES: FLIPPING, RENTING, AND REITS

Now that we have explored the different types of real estate properties, let's shift our attention to the strategies one can adopt to make money from these investments. Primarily, we will focus on three popular strategies in real estate investing: house flipping, renting, and investing in Real Estate Investment Trusts (REITs).

House Flipping

House flipping involves purchasing a property at a low price, often one in need of renovation or located in an up-and-coming neighborhood, then reselling it at a higher price to make a profit. This strategy requires a keen eye for properties with potential, a good understanding of renovation costs and real estate market trends, and an appetite for risk.

Successful flippers often have significant experience in real estate, construction, or home renovation. They're adept at identifying under-valued properties and accurately estimating renovation costs and the property's potential market value after improvements. Timing is crucial in house flipping as holding on to properties for longer than planned can significantly eat into profits due to ongoing financing, maintenance, and property tax costs. On the other hand, economic downturns can make it difficult to sell flipped properties at a profit.

Renting

Renting out a property, whether residential, commercial, or industrial, is one of the most common real estate investment strategies. In this approach, an investor purchases a property and then rents it out to tenants, collecting rental income over time. This strategy can provide a steady cash flow and potential property appreciation over time. However, it also involves ongoing property management tasks such as maintenance, finding and managing tenants, and dealing with legal issues like lease agreements and eviction processes.

Rental properties can provide a more steady and predictable income compared to flipping, making them popular with investors looking for consistent cash flow or supplemental income. The success of this strategy largely depends on the property's occupancy rate, the rental income it generates, and the ongoing expenses of maintaining the property. Therefore, it's crucial to accurately estimate these factors before investing.

Real Estate Investment Trusts (REITs)

For those who prefer a hands-off approach to real estate investing, REITs can be an attractive option. REITs are companies that own, operate, or finance income-generating real estate. Investors can buy shares of a REIT on the stock market, similar to how they would invest in any other publicly traded company.

One key advantage of REITs is that they allow investors to own a portion of real estate without having to buy an entire property. This provides the opportunity to invest in a diversified portfolio of real estate properties with a relatively small amount of capital. Moreover, since REITs are required to distribute at least 90% of their taxable income to shareholders as dividends, they can offer a steady income stream to investors.

However, since they are traded on the stock market, REITs are also subject to market volatility. The value of a REIT can go up and down based on overall market trends, which can affect the return on investment. Also, while REIT dividends can provide a steady income stream, they are generally taxed as ordinary income, which can be a disadvantage for some investors.

In summary, there are numerous strategies available to those interested in real estate investing, each with its unique risk and return profiles. House flipping can offer high returns but requires a good deal of expertise and risk tolerance. Renting out properties can provide steady income, but requires ongoing management effort. Finally, investing in REITs can be a passive way to invest in real estate but is subject to stock market volatility. By understanding these strategies and your personal investment goals and risk tolerance, you can choose the best strategy for your needs.

UNDERSTANDING THE REAL ESTATE MARKET: TOOLS FOR ANALYSIS

A key component of successful real estate investing lies in understanding and navigating the real estate market. Whether you're flipping houses, renting out properties, or investing in REITs, having a good grasp of the market is fundamental. This chapter will explore various tools and techniques to analyze and understand the real estate market.

Macro and Micro Market Analysis

Market analysis in real estate is often divided into two levels: macro and micro. Macro-level analysis involves examining broad economic trends, while micro-level analysis focuses on specific markets or properties.

On the macro level, investors should pay attention to national and regional economic trends, interest rates, employment levels, and population growth. Economic stability and growth often stimulate demand for real estate, leading to increased property values and rental rates. Changes in interest rates can affect the cost of borrowing money for real estate investments, and thus the overall profitability.

On the micro level, investors need to dig into local market conditions. This includes looking at local economic factors like job growth and unemployment rates, neighborhood demographics, real estate supply and demand, and recent sales and rental data. Other factors to consider are local infrastructure developments and zoning regulations, which can affect a property's appeal and future value.

Real Estate Market Indicators

Several key indicators can help investors understand the state of the real estate market:

- Sales Prices and Rental Rates: Trends in sales prices and rental rates can indicate whether a market is growing, stable, or declining. Steady growth in prices and rates typically suggests a healthy market.

- Inventory Levels: The number of properties for sale or rent in a market can signal whether it's a buyer's or seller's market. Low inventory levels often favor sellers, as buyers have fewer options, leading to increased prices.

- Days on Market (DOM): The average number of days properties stay listed before being sold or rented can also reveal market conditions. Shorter DOM often suggests strong demand and a seller's market.

- Vacancy Rates: For rental properties, vacancy rates are crucial. High vacancy rates may indicate a surplus of properties, which can put downward pressure on rental rates.

Online Tools and Data Sources

Many tools and data sources can help investors analyze real estate markets:

- Multiple Listing Service (MLS): This is a database used by real estate brokers to list and find properties for sale. MLS data can provide insights into local market conditions and trends.

- Real Estate Portals: Websites like Zillow, Realtor.com, and Trulia offer a wealth of information, including property listings, sales data, neighborhood demographics, and more.

- Government and Industry Reports: Reports from the U.S. Census Bureau, Bureau of Labor Statistics, Federal Reserve, and industry groups like the National Association of Realtors provide valuable data on national and regional economic and real estate trends.

- Local News and Reports: Local newspapers, business journals, and economic development reports can offer insights into local economic conditions, real estate developments, and trends.

Using Analysis Tools Effectively

While these tools and techniques can provide valuable insights, it's crucial to use them effectively. This involves:

- Comparing Data Over Time: Instead of focusing on a single point in time, look at trends over months or years. This can provide a clearer picture of the market direction.

- Comparing Local and National Data: National trends don't always reflect local conditions. Always compare local data with national trends to get a balanced perspective.

- Considering Different Data Points: Don't rely on a single indicator. Consider multiple data points to get a comprehensive view of the market.

Understanding the real estate market can seem overwhelming, given its complexity and the vast amount of data available. However, by using the right tools and strategies, you can significantly enhance your ability to make informed investment decisions.

Interpreting and Applying Market Analysis

Once you've gathered data and insights, it's essential to interpret and apply them to your investment decisions effectively. For example, if you're considering investing in rental properties in a specific neighborhood, and your analysis reveals low vacancy rates, high rental demand, and steady rent growth, this could suggest a favorable environment for your investment. However, if the same market shows signs of a significant increase in new rental supply, it could mean future competition, potentially leading to higher vacancy rates and lower rents.

Remember that no single tool or technique can provide a complete picture of the real estate market. Successful investors use a combination of these tools, along with their experience and intuition, to make investment decisions.

Risk Mitigation

Understanding market conditions and trends can also help you mitigate risk. By identifying potential challenges or changes in market conditions early, you can adapt your investment strategy accordingly. For example, if analysis suggests a market is becoming over-saturated with rental properties, you might decide to sell before rental rates decline, or diversify your investments into a different type of real estate or a different market.

Continuous Learning

Finally, keep in mind that understanding the real estate market isn't a one-time task. Markets continually evolve, influenced by a wide range of factors from changes in the economy and demographics, to shifts in consumer behavior and technological advancements. Therefore, ongoing learning and market analysis should be integral parts of your real estate investing journey.

In conclusion, understanding the real estate market is a critical aspect of successful real estate investing. While it involves considerable effort and continuous learning, having the right tools and techniques at your disposal can make the process much more manageable and rewarding. By analyzing both the macro and micro aspects of the market, keeping an eye on key market indicators, leveraging online tools and data sources, and applying your analysis effectively, you can make informed investment decisions and mitigate risks, setting the stage for successful real estate investments.

LOCATION, LOCATION, LOCATION: THE ART OF PROPERTY SELECTION

When it comes to real estate investing, one mantra stands above all: "Location, location, location." The importance of selecting the right location cannot be overstated. The right location can make or break your investment, determining its potential for growth, profitability, and long-term success. In this chapter, we delve into the art of property selection, exploring the key factors to consider when evaluating location for real estate investments.

Understanding the Significance of Location

Why is location so crucial in real estate? The location of a property directly impacts its value, rental demand, potential for appreciation, and overall desirability. A great property in a less desirable location may struggle to attract tenants or buyers, while an average property in a prime location can command higher rents and experience robust appreciation.

Factors to Consider when Evaluating Location

- Proximity to Amenities: Properties close to amenities such as schools, shopping centers, healthcare facilities, parks, and public transportation tend to be more desirable. Convenience is a significant factor for tenants and buyers alike.

- Neighborhood Quality: The quality of the neighborhood can greatly influence a property's value and desirability. Factors to consider include safety, cleanliness, access to public services, and the presence of community amenities.

- Economic and Job Growth: Areas with strong economic growth and job opportunities often experience increased demand for housing, leading to higher property values and rental demand.

- School Districts: Proximity to quality schools is a critical consideration for families and can significantly impact property values.

- Transportation Infrastructure: Easy access to major roads, highways, and public transportation can enhance a property's appeal, particularly in urban areas.

- Future Development Plans: Researching future development plans in the area can provide insights into potential growth and appreciation. Look for infrastructure projects, commercial developments, and zoning changes that may positively impact the location.

- Market Trends: Analyzing current market trends and future projections for the local real estate market is essential. Are property values appreciating? Is there high demand for rentals? Understanding the market dynamics can guide your decision-making process.

- Demographics: Consider the demographics of the area and the target market for your investment. Is the population growing? Are there specific demographics that are attracted to the location, such as young professionals, retirees, or families?

- Zoning and Land Use Regulations: Familiarize yourself with zoning laws and land use regulations in the area to ensure your investment aligns with the intended use and potential for future development.

- Competition: Evaluate the level of competition in the area. Are there many similar properties available for rent or sale? High competition may affect rental rates or resale potential.

Analyzing Location: Tools and Techniques

Several tools and techniques can assist in analyzing location for real estate investments:

- Local Market Reports: Research local market reports, including sales data, rental statistics, and economic indicators provided by real estate associations, government agencies, or reputable research firms.

- Online Tools: Utilize online platforms that offer property data, neighborhood information, crime statistics, school ratings, and demographic insights. Websites like Zillow, Redfin, and Trulia provide a wealth of information.

- Networking: Connect with local real estate professionals, investors, and property managers who have in-depth knowledge of the area. They can provide valuable insights into market conditions and trends.

- Site Visits and Observation: Conduct site visits to assess the neighborhood, observe local activity, and get a firsthand sense of the location's desirability and potential.

Balancing Location with Investment Goals

While a prime location is important, it's essential to balance it with your investment goals and budget. The ideal location for one investor may not be the same for another, as investment strategies and objectives can vary widely. Consider the following factors when balancing location with your investment goals:

- Affordability: Prime locations often come with a higher price tag. Assess whether the potential returns and growth prospects align with the investment's cost. Sometimes, investing in a slightly less desirable location can offer better affordability and potential for higher returns.

- Risk Tolerance: Risk tolerance varies among investors. Some may be willing to take on higher risk in emerging or transitional neighborhoods for the potential of greater returns, while others may prefer more stable, established areas. Assess your risk tolerance and align it with the location's risk profile.

- Investment Strategy: Different investment strategies may require different location considerations. For example, if you're focused on long-term appreciation, selecting a property in an area with anticipated growth and development may be more important. If cash flow is your priority, choosing a location with high rental demand and strong rental rates may be key.

- Exit Strategy: Consider your exit strategy when evaluating location. Are you planning to hold the property for a long time and benefit from appreciation, or are you aiming to sell quickly for a profit? The location's potential for appreciation and market liquidity should align with your desired exit strategy.

Special Considerations for International Investments

Investing in real estate abroad requires additional considerations due to the unfamiliarity with local markets and regulations. Some key factors to address when investing internationally include:

- Legal and Regulatory Environment: Familiarize yourself with local laws, regulations, and restrictions on property ownership, foreign investment, and taxation. Seek professional advice to ensure compliance.

- Economic and Political Stability: Assess the country's economic and political stability, as these factors can influence property values, rental demand, and the overall investment climate.

- Cultural Considerations: Understand cultural nuances that can impact the real estate market, such as preferred property types, rental practices, and local preferences.

- Local Partnerships: Building relationships with local partners, real estate agents, or property managers who have knowledge and experience in the target market can provide valuable guidance and support.

In conclusion, selecting the right location is a critical component of successful real estate investing. By thoroughly evaluating factors such as proximity to amenities, neighborhood quality, economic conditions, transportation infrastructure, and market trends, you can make informed decisions that align with your investment goals. Utilizing tools, conducting thorough research, and networking with local professionals will enhance your understanding of the location and minimize risks. Balancing location with your investment strategy, risk tolerance, and budget is essential for long-term success. Whether Investing locally or internationally, thorough due diligence and adapting to the specific considerations of each market will help you make strategic property selections and maximize your investment potential. Remember, when it comes to real estate investing, location truly is the foundation for success.

FINANCING YOUR INVESTMENTS: LOANS, MORTGAGES, AND MORE

Real estate investments often require substantial capital, and securing appropriate financing is a crucial aspect of successful investing. In this chapter, we explore various financing options available to investors, including loans, mortgages, and alternative methods, along with the factors to consider when evaluating and obtaining financing for your real estate investments.

Assessing Your Financial Position

Before diving into financing options, it's important to assess your financial position and determine how much capital you have available for investments. Evaluate your personal savings, investments, and access to additional funds. Understanding your financial capabilities will help guide your financing decisions and determine the type and size of investments you can pursue.

Traditional Financing Options

- Conventional Mortgage: A conventional mortgage is a popular option for financing residential properties. It involves borrowing money from a bank or financial institution, where the property itself serves as collateral for the loan. Conventional mortgages typically require a down payment, and the interest rate and terms depend on factors such as credit history, income, and the loan-to-value ratio.

- Commercial Mortgage: For commercial properties, including retail spaces, office buildings, or industrial facilities, a commercial mortgage is commonly used. These loans are tailored for business purposes, often with different terms and qualification criteria than conventional mortgages.

- Hard Money Loan: Hard money loans are short-term, asset-based loans provided by private individuals or companies. They are typically used for fix-and-flip projects or when traditional financing options are not available due to credit or property condition. Hard money loans often have higher interest rates and shorter terms but provide faster access to capital.

- Portfolio Loans: Some banks or credit unions offer portfolio loans, which allow investors to finance multiple investment properties within a single loan. These loans can provide flexibility and simplify the financing process for those with multiple properties.

Government-Backed Financing Options

- Federal Housing Administration (FHA) Loans: FHA loans are insured by the Federal Housing Administration and are designed to make homeownership more accessible. They offer lower down payment requirements and more flexible qualification criteria, making them suitable for first-time homebuyers.

- Veterans Affairs (VA) Loans: VA loans are available to eligible veterans and provide favorable terms, including no down payment requirement and competitive interest rates. They are guaranteed by the U.S. Department of Veterans Affairs.

- United States Department of Agriculture (USDA) Loans: USDA loans are aimed at promoting rural development and homeownership. They offer attractive terms, including zero down payment options, to individuals purchasing properties in eligible rural areas.

Alternative Financing Methods

- Seller Financing: In seller financing, the property owner acts as the lender, offering financing directly to the buyer. This can be a viable option when traditional financing is challenging to obtain or when the seller is motivated to sell quickly. Terms and conditions, including interest rates and repayment schedules, are negotiated between the buyer and seller.

- Private Lenders and Partnerships: Private lenders and partnerships are alternative sources of financing where individuals or groups provide funds for real estate investments in exchange for a return on their investment. These arrangements often involve negotiated terms and can be useful for investors with limited access to traditional financing.

- Crowdfunding: Crowdfunding platforms have emerged as an alternative financing method for real estate investments. Through these platforms, investors can pool their funds to invest in various properties or projects. Crowdfunding can offer accessibility and diversification but requires careful evaluation of the platform, investment opportunities, and associated risks.

Factors to Consider when Evaluating Financing Options

- Interest Rates: Interest rates significantly impact the overall cost of borrowing. Compare rates from multiple lenders to secure the most favorable terms.

- Loan Terms: Consider the duration of the loan and repayment terms. Longer loan terms may result in lower monthly payments but can increase the total interest paid over time.

- Down Payment Requirements: Evaluate the down payment requirements of different financing options. Higher down payments can lead to lower interest rates and reduce the loan amount, but they may require more upfront capital.

- Closing Costs and Fees: Consider the associated closing costs, origination fees, and other charges that come with obtaining financing. These can vary between lenders and impact the overall cost of the loan.

- Qualification Criteria: Understand the qualification criteria for each financing option. Factors such as credit history, income, and debt-to-income ratio can influence your eligibility for certain loans.

- Flexibility: Assess the flexibility of the financing option. Some loans may have prepayment penalties or limited flexibility in terms of refinancing or modifying the loan terms.

- Risk Management: Consider the impact of the financing option on your risk exposure. High leverage or variable interest rates can increase the risks associated with the investment.

- Relationship with Lenders: Building relationships with lenders can be beneficial for future financing needs. Consider the reputation, responsiveness, and customer service of potential lenders.

Loan Application and Documentation

When applying for financing, be prepared to provide documentation such as personal financial statements, tax returns, bank statements, and property-related information. Lenders will evaluate your financial capacity, creditworthiness, and the value and potential of the property being financed.

It is advisable to work with a mortgage broker or loan officer who can guide you through the application process, help you compare offers, and assist in gathering the necessary documentation.

Mitigating Financing Risks

While financing can be an effective tool for real estate investments, it also comes with risks. Here are some ways to mitigate these risks:

- Thorough Due Diligence: Conduct comprehensive due diligence on the property, including market analysis, property inspection, and evaluation of rental potential or resale value. This helps ensure that the investment aligns with the financing terms.

- Cash Reserves: Maintain cash reserves to cover unexpected expenses, vacancies, or changes in market conditions. This provides a cushion to manage potential financial challenges.

- Proper Cash Flow Analysis: Conduct a thorough cash flow analysis to ensure that the investment generates sufficient income to cover financing costs, including loan payments, interest, taxes, insurance, and maintenance expenses.

- Review Financing Terms: Carefully review and understand the terms and conditions of the loan agreement. Pay attention to interest rate adjustments, balloon payments, or other potential risks associated with the loan structure.

- Conservative Debt-to-Equity Ratio: Avoid over-leveraging by maintaining a conservative debt-to-equity ratio. This helps mitigate the risk of financial strain if property values or rental income decline.

In conclusion, financing plays a significant role in real estate investments, providing the necessary capital to acquire and develop properties. Understanding the various financing options available, along with their associated terms, interest rates, and requirements, is crucial in making informed decisions. Evaluate your financial position, explore traditional and alternative financing methods, and consider factors such as interest rates, loan terms, and qualification criteria. Mitigate financing risks through proper due diligence, cash reserves, and conservative financial planning. By aligning financing with your investment goals and mitigating risks, you can effectively leverage capital to maximize the potential of your real estate investments.

THE POWER OF LEVERAGE IN REAL ESTATE INVESTING

Leverage is a powerful tool that has the potential to greatly amplify the returns and growth of real estate investments. In this chapter, we explore the concept of leverage, its benefits and risks, and how it can be effectively utilized in real estate investing.

Understanding Leverage

Leverage in real estate investing refers to using borrowed funds, such as a mortgage or loan, to acquire an investment property. It allows investors to control a more substantial asset with a smaller amount of their own capital. Leverage is made possible by the fact that real estate is a tangible asset with inherent value that can serve as collateral for borrowing.

Benefits of Leverage

- Increased Buying Power: Leverage enables investors to purchase properties that may be beyond their immediate financial capacity. By leveraging funds from lenders, investors can acquire properties that have the potential for higher returns and greater appreciation.

- Enhanced Return on Investment (ROI): When the property value appreciates, the investor's return is calculated based on the property's total value, not just the initial investment. This amplifies the return on the investor's own capital. For example, if an investor puts down $50,000 on a $200,000 property and the property appreciates by 10%, the investor's return is 40% ($20,000) on their initial $50,000 investment.

- Cash Flow Generation: Leverage allows investors to generate cash flow from rental income while using borrowed funds. The rental income can help cover financing costs and expenses, leaving the investor with positive cash flow.

- Diversification Opportunities: With leverage, investors can spread their capital across multiple properties, diversifying their investment portfolio. This reduces risk and provides exposure to different real estate markets and property types.

Calculating Return on Investment with Leverage

To understand the impact of leverage on return on investment (ROI), consider the following example:

- Scenario A: An investor purchases a property worth $500,000 using their own funds and experiences a 5% increase in property value. Their ROI would be 5%.

- Scenario B: Another investor purchases the same property using $100,000 of their own funds and borrows the remaining $400,000. They also experience a 5% increase in property value. In this case, their ROI would be 25% ($100,000 profit on a $400,000 investment).

Comparing the two scenarios, it is clear that leveraging funds has the potential to significantly increase ROI, allowing investors to achieve higher returns on their own capital.

Risks and Considerations

While leverage offers great potential benefits, it is important to be aware of the risks and exercise caution when utilizing it:

- Increased Financial Risk: Borrowing funds introduces financial risk. If property values decline, rental income decreases, or interest rates rise significantly, the investor may face challenges in meeting their financial obligations.

- Debt Servicing Costs: Borrowing funds comes with interest payments and other associated costs, which must be factored into cash flow projections. Adequate cash flow should be generated to cover these costs, ensuring the investment remains profitable.

- Market Fluctuations: Real estate markets can experience fluctuations in property values and rental demand. Investors must carefully evaluate market conditions and potential risks when utilizing leverage.

- Loan Terms and Interest Rates: The terms of the loan, including interest rates, repayment schedules, and fees, should be thoroughly analyzed. Understanding these terms is crucial in assessing the long-term financial impact of leverage on the investment.

- Personal Financial Situation: Investors should assess their own financial situation, risk tolerance, and ability to handle debt before using leverage. A comprehensive financial plan should be in place to ensure that leveraging funds aligns with personal financial goals and capabilities.

Strategies for Effective Use of Leverage

- Conservative Loan-to-Value (LTV) Ratio: Maintaining a conservative loan-to-value ratio helps mitigate risk. Avoid over-leveraging by ensuring that the loan amount is reasonable in relation to the property's value and potential cash flow.

- Cash Reserves: Maintain cash reserves to handle unexpected expenses, periods of vacancy, or fluctuations in the real estate market. This provides a safety net to manage financial obligations associated with the leverage.

- Thorough Due Diligence: Conduct comprehensive due diligence on the investment property, including market analysis, property inspection, and evaluation of rental potential. Ensure that the property's cash flow and potential for appreciation justify the leverage utilized.

- Consider Multiple Financing Options: Explore various financing options to find the most favorable terms and interest rates. Compare offers from different lenders to secure the most beneficial financing arrangement.

- Risk Management and Portfolio Diversification: Utilize leverage strategically as part of a diversified investment portfolio. Spreading leverage across different properties or markets can help mitigate risk and balance the potential rewards.

- Long-Term Perspective: Leverage is most effective when viewed as a long-term investment strategy. Real estate investments generally require time to appreciate in value and generate substantial returns. Consider the long-term potential of the property and its market before utilizing leverage.

Professional Guidance and Risk Assessment

Seeking professional guidance from real estate advisors, financial planners, and mortgage professionals can provide valuable insights into the risks and benefits of leveraging. These experts can help assess your personal financial situation, evaluate investment opportunities, and determine the most suitable financing options based on your goals and risk tolerance.

Additionally, it is essential to conduct a thorough risk assessment for each investment, considering factors such as market conditions, rental demand, and potential cash flow. Careful analysis and risk mitigation strategies will help safeguard your investments and minimize the potential downsides of utilizing leverage.

Conclusion

Leverage is a powerful tool in real estate investing that allows investors to maximize returns and access larger investments with a smaller amount of personal capital. By effectively utilizing leverage, investors can benefit from increased buying power, enhanced ROI, cash flow generation, and portfolio diversification.

However, leveraging funds also carries risks, including financial obligations, market fluctuations, and personal financial exposure. It is crucial to carefully assess your financial position, conduct thorough due diligence, and consider the long-term implications of leverage on your investment strategy.

By understanding the benefits and risks associated with leverage and implementing risk mitigation strategies, investors can harness the power of leverage to achieve their real estate investment goals and build wealth over time.

LEGAL ASPECTS OF REAL ESTATE: WHAT EVERY INVESTOR SHOULD KNOW

Real estate investing involves various legal considerations that can significantly impact the success of your investments. Understanding the legal aspects is essential for protecting your interests, complying with regulations, and ensuring a smooth investment process. In this chapter, we explore key legal aspects of real estate investing that every investor should know.

Contracts and Agreements

Contracts and agreements play a vital role in real estate transactions. Whether you're buying or selling a property, entering into a lease agreement, or forming partnerships, it's important to have legally binding agreements in place. Here are some key contract and agreement types to be aware of:

- Purchase and Sale Agreement: This contract outlines the terms and conditions of a property purchase. It includes details such as the purchase price, financing arrangements, contingencies, and closing dates.

- Lease Agreement: A lease agreement establishes the terms of a rental arrangement between the landlord (property owner) and the tenant. It covers aspects like rental payments, lease duration, maintenance responsibilities, and termination conditions.

- Partnership Agreements: If you're investing with partners, a partnership agreement clarifies the roles, responsibilities, and profit-sharing arrangements among the partners. It also addresses potential disputes and exit strategies.

- Construction Contracts: When undertaking construction or renovation projects, construction contracts outline the scope of work, timelines, payment terms, and dispute resolution procedures between the investor and contractors.

Working with legal professionals, such as real estate attorneys, can ensure that contracts and agreements are properly drafted, reviewed, and tailored to protect your interests.

Property Ownership and Title

Understanding property ownership and title is fundamental to real estate investing. Key aspects to consider include:

- Title Search and Title Insurance: Conducting a title search is crucial before purchasing a property to ensure that the title is clear of any liens, encumbrances, or legal issues. Title insurance protects against potential defects in the title that may arise in the future.

- Deeds: Deeds are legal documents that transfer ownership of a property from one party to another. The type of deed used depends on the specific transaction, such as a warranty deed, quitclaim deed, or grant deed.

- Ownership Structures: Choosing the appropriate ownership structure is important. Options include sole ownership, partnerships, limited liability companies (LLCs), and corporations. Each structure has different legal implications, liability protections, and tax considerations.

- Easements and Rights of Way: Easements grant others the right to use a portion of your property for specific purposes, such as access to public roads or utilities. Understanding existing easements or potential rights of way is critical when assessing the property's value and potential future development.

Consulting with real estate attorneys and title professionals can help ensure that property ownership is properly established, and potential legal issues are addressed.

Real Estate Regulations and Compliance

Real estate investments are subject to various regulations at the local, state, and federal levels. It's crucial to comply with these regulations to avoid legal penalties and protect your investment. Key areas of regulation to be aware of include:

- Zoning and Land Use Regulations: Zoning laws dictate how properties can be used, such as residential, commercial, or industrial purposes. Familiarize yourself with zoning regulations to ensure that your investment aligns with the intended use and potential for future development.

- Environmental Regulations: Environmental regulations address potential hazards or contamination issues on the property. Conducting environmental assessments, such as Phase I and Phase II environmental site assessments, can help identify any environmental risks.

- Fair Housing Laws: Fair housing laws prohibit discrimination based on race, color, religion, sex, national origin, disability, or familial status in the rental or sale of properties. Familiarize yourself with fair housing laws to ensure compliance in all aspects of your real estate transactions.

- Tenant and Landlord Laws: Understanding tenant and landlord laws is crucial when leasing out properties. These laws govern aspects such as security deposits, eviction processes, rent increases, and tenant rights. Complying with these laws protects both the landlord and the tenant and helps maintain a positive landlord-tenant relationship.

- Tax Regulations: Real estate investments have tax implications, including property taxes, capital gains taxes, and potential tax incentives for certain types of investments or properties. Consult with tax professionals to understand the tax obligations and opportunities related to your real estate investments.

Staying updated on changes in regulations and seeking legal advice when necessary will help you navigate the complexities of real estate regulations and ensure compliance.

Risk Management and Insurance

Managing risk is an integral part of real estate investing. Here are key aspects of risk management and insurance to consider:

- Liability Protection: Real estate investments carry inherent risks, such as property damage, accidents, or legal claims. Structuring your investments within limited liability entities, such as LLCs, can help shield personal assets from potential liabilities.

- Insurance Coverage: Adequate insurance coverage is essential to protect your investment. Consider property insurance, liability insurance, and additional coverage like flood insurance or landlord insurance, depending on the property type and specific risks involved.

- Risk Assessment: Conduct thorough risk assessments for each investment property. Identify potential hazards, perform due diligence on property conditions, and implement risk mitigation strategies, such as property inspections and maintenance protocols.

- Legal Dispute Resolution: In the event of legal disputes, it's important to be prepared with dispute resolution mechanisms. Consider including arbitration or mediation clauses in contracts to resolve disputes without resorting to costly litigation.

Working closely with legal and insurance professionals can help identify and mitigate potential risks, protect your investments, and minimize the impact of unforeseen legal issues.

Conclusion

Understanding the legal aspects of real estate investing is essential for safeguarding your investments, complying with regulations, and maximizing the potential for success. From contracts and agreements to property ownership, regulations, risk management, and insurance, each aspect plays a crucial role in your real estate journey. By working with legal professionals, conducting thorough due diligence, and staying informed on changes in regulations, you can navigate the legal complexities and make informed decisions that protect your interests and support your real estate investment goals. Remember, legal compliance is not only a legal requirement but also a fundamental aspect of ethical and responsible real estate investing.

PROPERTY MANAGEMENT 101: MAINTAINING YOUR INVESTMENT

Effective property management is essential for maintaining the value, maximizing the returns, and ensuring the long-term success of your real estate investments. Property management involves overseeing the day-to-day operations, maintenance, and tenant relations of your properties. In this chapter, we delve into the fundamentals of property management and provide key insights and strategies for maintaining your investment.

The Role of Property Management

Property management encompasses a wide range of responsibilities to ensure the smooth operation of your real estate investments. Some of the key roles and responsibilities of property management include:

- Tenant Acquisition and Screening: Property managers handle advertising vacancies, screening potential tenants, conducting background checks, and executing lease agreements.

- Rent Collection: Property managers are responsible for collecting rent, enforcing lease terms, and addressing any late payments or delinquencies.

- Maintenance and Repairs: Property managers oversee routine maintenance tasks, repairs, and property inspections to ensure that the property remains in good condition and complies with safety and habitability standards.

- Tenant Relations and Conflict Resolution: Property managers act as a point of contact for tenants, addressing their concerns, resolving disputes, and maintaining positive relationships to promote tenant satisfaction and retention.

- Financial Management: Property managers handle financial aspects, including budgeting, accounting, expense tracking, and financial reporting to ensure proper financial management of the property.

- Compliance and Legal Obligations: Property managers ensure compliance with local, state, and federal regulations, including fair housing laws, building codes, health and safety standards, and property-specific regulations.

Selecting a Property Manager

When it comes to property management, you have the option to self-manage or hire a professional property management company. Consider the following factors when selecting a property manager:

- Expertise and Experience: Look for property managers with extensive experience in managing properties similar to yours. A property manager with knowledge of local market dynamics, tenant relations, and maintenance practices can provide valuable insights and ensure effective management.

- Reputation and References: Research the reputation of property management companies or individuals by checking online reviews, seeking references, and contacting their current or past clients. A good reputation indicates professionalism, reliability, and tenant satisfaction.

- Services and Fees: Assess the range of services offered by the property manager and ensure they align with your needs. Inquire about their fee structure, including management fees and any additional charges, to evaluate the cost-effectiveness of their services.

- Communication and Accessibility: Effective communication is crucial for a successful property management relationship. Ensure that the property manager is responsive, maintains regular communication channels, and provides timely updates on property-related matters.

Maintenance and Repairs

Proper maintenance and prompt repairs are essential for preserving the value of your investment and ensuring tenant satisfaction. Here are some key considerations for effective maintenance and repair management:

- Preventive Maintenance: Implement a proactive approach to maintenance by conducting regular inspections and addressing minor issues before they escalate. Regularly inspect the property's systems, such as HVAC, plumbing, and electrical, to identify potential maintenance needs.

- Vendor Management: Establish relationships with reliable contractors, vendors, and service providers for maintenance and repair tasks. Obtain multiple quotes, evaluate their qualifications, and ensure they are licensed, insured, and experienced in the specific type of work required.

- Emergency Response Plan: Have an emergency response plan in place to address urgent maintenance issues such as leaks, electrical failures, or security concerns. Maintain a list of emergency contacts, including contractors and service providers available 24/7.

- Tenant Communication: Maintain open lines of communication with tenants regarding maintenance procedures, reporting mechanisms, and expected response times. Promptly address tenant maintenance requests and keep them informed of the progress and resolution of their issues.

- Record-Keeping: Maintain thorough records of all maintenance and repair activities, including work orders, invoices, warranties, and inspection reports. This documentation is essential for tracking expenses, warranty claims, and ensuring compliance with legal and insurance requirements.

- Budgeting for Maintenance: Set aside funds in your budget specifically for property maintenance and repairs. Having a dedicated maintenance budget allows for timely repairs and helps prevent deferred maintenance, which can lead to more significant issues and higher costs in the long run.

Tenant Relations and Retention

Tenant satisfaction is crucial for maintaining a stable rental income stream and reducing vacancies. Consider the following strategies to foster positive tenant relations and encourage tenant retention:

- Effective Communication: Establish clear communication channels with tenants, providing multiple methods for them to contact you or the property manager. Respond promptly to their inquiries, concerns, and maintenance requests to demonstrate your commitment to their satisfaction.

- Respectful and Fair Treatment: Treat tenants with respect, fairness, and professionalism. Address any issues or disputes promptly and in accordance with the lease agreement and applicable laws. Consistent and fair treatment contributes to a positive tenant experience.

- Tenant Engagement: Promote a sense of community and tenant engagement by organizing social events, implementing amenities, or creating shared spaces within the property. Encouraging tenant interaction can contribute to a positive living environment and foster a sense of belonging.

- Responsive Maintenance: Timely and efficient resolution of maintenance issues is crucial for tenant satisfaction. Ensure that maintenance requests are addressed promptly, and repairs are completed to the tenants' satisfaction.

- Lease Renewal Incentives: Consider offering lease renewal incentives, such as rent discounts, upgrade options, or lease term flexibility, to encourage tenants to renew their leases. Retaining reliable, long-term tenants reduces turnover costs and maintains a consistent rental income.

Legal Compliance and Risk Management

Compliance with legal and regulatory requirements is essential for protecting your investment and avoiding potential legal issues. Consider the following aspects of legal compliance and risk management:

- Fair Housing Laws: Familiarize yourself with fair housing laws and ensure compliance to prevent discrimination in tenant selection and management practices.

- Lease Agreements: Ensure that lease agreements are legally sound, comprehensive, and comply with local laws and regulations. Include provisions that protect your interests, address tenant responsibilities, and clearly define the rights and obligations of both parties.

- Insurance Coverage: Obtain appropriate insurance coverage for your investment property. This may include property insurance, liability insurance, and landlord insurance, depending on the property type and specific risks involved. Regularly review and update your insurance coverage to mitigate potential risks.

- Risk Assessment: Conduct regular risk assessments to identify potential hazards or liabilities associated with the property. Implement appropriate risk management strategies, such as maintaining safety measures, conducting inspections, and addressing potential security risks.

- Legal Advice: Consult with real estate attorneys or legal professionals to ensure compliance with local, state, and federal laws. Seek their guidance on legal aspects of property management, lease agreements, eviction procedures, and other legal obligations.

Conclusion

Effective property management is vital for maintaining the value and maximizing the returns of your real estate investments. By understanding the roles and responsibilities of property management, selecting reliable property managers or establishing efficient self-management practices, and prioritizing maintenance, tenant relations, and legal compliance, you can ensure the long-term success of your investment properties. Effective property management contributes to tenant satisfaction, reduces vacancies, and minimizes risks, ultimately leading to a profitable and well-maintained real estate portfolio.

RISK MANAGEMENT: AVOIDING COMMON PITFALLS

Real estate investing comes with inherent risks, and effective risk management is crucial to protect your investments and maximize their potential. In this chapter, we delve into the key aspects of risk management and provide strategies for avoiding common pitfalls that can jeopardize your real estate portfolio.

Identifying and Assessing Risks

The first step in risk management is identifying and assessing potential risks associated with your real estate investments. Common risks in real estate investing include:

- Market Risk: Fluctuations in the real estate market, such as changes in property values, rental demand, or economic conditions, can impact the profitability of your investments.

- Financing Risk: Risks associated with borrowing funds, including interest rate changes, inability to secure financing, or loan default.

- Operational Risk: Challenges related to property management, such as maintenance issues, tenant turnover, or unexpected expenses.

- Legal and Regulatory Risk: Non-compliance with laws and regulations, lawsuits, zoning issues, or disputes with tenants or other stakeholders.

- Environmental Risk: Environmental hazards, contamination, or natural disasters that can affect the value or usability of the property.

- Insurance and Liability Risk: Inadequate insurance coverage, liability claims, or property damage that can result in financial loss.

By thoroughly assessing these risks, you can develop strategies to mitigate them and make informed decisions.

Mitigating Risks in Real Estate Investing

- Diversification: Diversifying your real estate portfolio across different property types, locations, and investment strategies can help spread risks. A diverse portfolio is less susceptible to the impact of a single property's poor performance or a specific market downturn.

- Thorough Due Diligence: Conduct comprehensive due diligence before making an investment. This includes evaluating the property's location, market dynamics, rental potential, and financial projections. Investigate the property's condition, legal history, and any potential environmental issues.

- Financial Analysis and Cash Flow Management: Perform thorough financial analysis, including cash flow projections, to ensure that your investment generates sufficient income to cover expenses and debt obligations. Implement a cash flow management plan to maintain sufficient reserves for unexpected expenses or periods of vacancy.

- Conservative Financing: Avoid over-leveraging and maintain a conservative debt-to-equity ratio. By not relying excessively on borrowed funds, you reduce the risk of financial strain in case of market downturns or unexpected expenses.

- Maintain Adequate Insurance Coverage: Obtain comprehensive insurance coverage for your properties, including property insurance, liability insurance, and any additional coverage needed for specific risks. Regularly review and update your insurance policies to ensure they adequately protect your investments.

- Strong Property Management: Effective property management is crucial for risk mitigation. Select experienced property managers or adopt efficient self-management practices to ensure proper maintenance, tenant screening, and rent collection. Promptly address maintenance issues and foster positive tenant relations to reduce potential risks.

- Compliance with Laws and Regulations: Stay up-to-date with local, state, and federal laws and regulations governing real estate investments. Ensure compliance with fair housing laws, building codes, health and safety standards, and other applicable regulations.

- Continuous Monitoring and Evaluation: Regularly monitor and evaluate the performance of your investments. Stay informed about market trends, property values, and local economic conditions. This allows you to identify potential risks and take proactive measures to mitigate them.

- Professional Advice and Networking: Seek advice from experienced professionals, such as real estate attorneys, accountants, and financial advisors. Their expertise can help you navigate legal complexities, tax implications, and financial planning. Networking with other investors can also provide valuable insights and risk management strategies.

Learning from Common Pit falls

Learning from common pitfalls that other real estate investors have experienced can help you avoid similar mistakes. Here are some common pitfalls and strategies to mitigate them:

- Overestimating Returns: Avoid the pitfall of overestimating potential returns on investment properties. Conduct thorough market research, analyze comparable sales and rental data, and factor in all expenses, including financing costs, maintenance, and property management fees. Be realistic in your projections and conservative in your assumptions.

- Insufficient Due Diligence: Inadequate due diligence can lead to unexpected issues and financial losses. Take the time to thoroughly assess the property, conduct property inspections, review documentation, and verify information provided by sellers or agents. Engage professionals, such as real estate attorneys, appraisers, and inspectors, to assist in the due diligence process.

- Lack of Financial Reserves: Insufficient cash reserves can leave you vulnerable to unexpected expenses or periods of vacancy. Maintain an emergency fund to cover unforeseen repairs, maintenance, or prolonged vacancies. A general rule of thumb is to have at least three to six months' worth of expenses set aside.

- Poor Property Management: Ineffective property management can lead to tenant issues, high turnover rates, and inadequate maintenance. Carefully select reliable property managers or educate yourself on effective self-management practices. Regularly communicate with tenants, promptly address their concerns, and proactively manage maintenance and repairs.

- Ignoring Market Trends: Failing to stay informed about market trends and shifts can result in poor investment decisions. Stay updated on local market conditions, economic indicators, and demographic trends. Monitor factors such as job growth, population changes, and development plans that can impact property values and rental demand.

- Ignoring Legal and Regulatory Compliance: Non-compliance with laws and regulations can lead to legal troubles and financial losses. Stay informed about fair housing laws, lease regulations, property maintenance requirements, and zoning ordinances. Engage legal professionals to ensure compliance and mitigate legal risks.

- Neglecting Risk Management Strategies: Failing to implement risk management strategies can leave your investments vulnerable. Identify potential risks, create contingency plans, and maintain adequate insurance coverage. Regularly review your risk management strategies and adapt them as needed based on changes in market conditions or property-specific factors.

- Overreliance on a Single Property or Market: Relying too heavily on a single property or market can expose you to significant risks. Diversify your portfolio across different property types, locations, and markets. This spreads the risks and allows you to benefit from the potential of multiple investments.

- Lack of Exit Strategy: Failing to have a clear exit strategy can limit your flexibility and potentially lead to financial losses. Define your investment goals and determine exit strategies such as selling, refinancing, or transitioning to a different investment strategy. Regularly review and update your exit strategies based on market conditions and changes in your investment objectives.

By learning from these common pitfalls and implementing effective risk management strategies, you can minimize potential risks, protect your investments, and increase the likelihood of long-term success in real estate investing.

Conclusion

Risk management is a vital aspect of real estate investing. By identifying and assessing potential risks, implementing effective risk mitigation strategies, and learning from common pitfalls, you can protect your investments and enhance their profitability. Thorough due diligence, conservative financial analysis, strong property management, legal compliance, and continuous monitoring are key components of successful risk management. By actively managing risks, you position yourself for long-term success and the ability to navigate challenges that may arise in the dynamic real estate market.

TAX IMPLICATIONS OF REAL ESTATE INVESTING

Understanding the tax implications of real estate investing is essential for maximizing your returns and optimizing your overall financial strategy. In this chapter, we explore the key tax considerations that real estate investors should be aware of, including deductions, depreciation, capital gains, and entity structures.

Rental Income and Deductions

Rental income generated from investment properties is subject to taxation. However, there are several deductions that real estate investors can take advantage of to reduce their taxable income:

- Operating Expenses: Deductible operating expenses include property management fees, repairs and maintenance, insurance premiums, property taxes, utilities, and advertising costs.

- Mortgage Interest: The interest paid on mortgages or loans used to finance the acquisition or improvement of investment properties is generally tax-deductible. This deduction can significantly reduce taxable income.

- Depreciation: Depreciation allows investors to deduct a portion of the property's cost over its useful life. Residential properties are typically depreciated over 27.5 years, while commercial properties are depreciated over 39 years. Depreciation can provide substantial tax benefits, as it is a non-cash deduction.

- Home Office Deduction: If you have a dedicated space in your home used exclusively for your real estate investment activities, you may qualify for a home office deduction. This deduction allows you to deduct a portion of your home-related expenses, such as mortgage interest, property taxes, utilities, and insurance.

- Travel and Transportation: Expenses related to travel and transportation for real estate investment purposes, such as visiting properties, meeting with tenants or professionals, and attending industry conferences, may be deductible. Keep detailed records and consult with a tax professional to determine the eligibility of these deductions.

- Legal and Professional Fees: Fees paid to attorneys, accountants, and other professionals for real estate-related services are generally tax-deductible. This includes fees for tax preparation, legal advice, and property management services.

Capital Gains and 1031 Exchanges

Capital gains tax is applicable when you sell an investment property for a profit. The tax rate on capital gains depends on the holding period and your income tax bracket. However, there are strategies to defer or minimize capital gains tax:

- 1031 Exchange: A 1031 exchange allows you to defer capital gains tax by reinvesting the proceeds from the sale of one investment property into a like-kind property. By complying with specific rules and timelines, you can defer the recognition of capital gains and continue to grow your real estate portfolio.

- Capital Gain Exclusion: If you sell a primary residence that you have lived in for at least two out of the past five years, you may qualify for a capital gain exclusion. The exclusion allows individuals to exclude up to $250,000 of capital gains from their taxable income ($500,000 for married couples filing jointly).

- Long-Term vs. Short-Term Capital Gains: Capital gains on assets held for more than one year are generally taxed at lower rates than short-term gains. Long-term capital gains tax rates are based on your income tax bracket and can provide tax savings for investors who hold properties for an extended period.

Entity Structures and Tax Benefits

Choosing the right entity structure for your real estate investments can have significant tax implications. Here are some common entity structures and their associated tax benefits:

- Sole Proprietorship: The simplest and most common entity structure, where an individual owns and operates the investment property. While there are no separate tax filings, income and expenses are reported on the owner's personal tax return.

- Limited Liability Company (LLC): An LLC offers liability protection for the owner(s) and flexibility in terms of taxation. By default, an LLC is considered a pass-through entity, meaning that profits and losses are passed through to the individual owners and reported on their personal tax returns. This structure allows for flexibility in allocating income and deductions among the owners.

- Partnerships: Similar to an LLC, a partnership is a pass-through entity where income and losses flow through to the partners. Partnerships offer flexibility in allocating profits and losses among partners based on their ownership percentages.

- S Corporations: An S Corporation is another pass-through entity that provides liability protection and potential tax benefits. It allows for the allocation of income and deductions among shareholders, reducing self-employment taxes for the shareholders.

- Real Estate Investment Trusts (REITs): REITs are entities that own and operate income-generating real estate properties. They offer significant tax advantages, such as the ability to avoid corporate-level taxation by distributing at least 90% of their taxable income to shareholders in the form of dividends.

Choosing the right entity structure depends on various factors, including the size and complexity of your real estate portfolio, your long-term goals, liability protection needs, and potential tax benefits. It's essential to consult with a tax professional or an attorney specializing in real estate taxation to determine the most suitable entity structure for your specific circumstances.

Tax Planning and Professional Guidance

Proactive tax planning is crucial for real estate investors to maximize tax benefits and optimize their overall financial strategy. Here are some strategies to consider:

- Engage a Tax Professional: Real estate taxation can be complex, and tax laws and regulations are subject to change. Working with a qualified tax professional who specializes in real estate taxation ensures that you stay compliant, take advantage of available deductions, and make informed decisions that align with your financial goals.

- Maintain Detailed Records: Keep thorough records of income, expenses, and property-related transactions. Accurate and well-organized records will simplify tax preparation, support deductions and credits, and provide documentation in case of an audit.

- Plan for Depreciation Recapture: When you sell a property and have claimed depreciation deductions, a portion of the gain may be subject to depreciation recapture tax. Understanding the implications of depreciation recapture and planning for it can help you mitigate the tax impact.

- Evaluate Tax Credits and Incentives: Research tax credits and incentives that may be available for specific real estate investments, such as historic rehabilitation tax credits or energy-efficient property credits. These incentives can reduce your overall tax liability and increase your after-tax returns.

- Stay Updated on Tax Laws: Tax laws and regulations related to real estate investing can change over time. Stay informed about new tax provisions, deductions, and reporting requirements that may impact your investments. Regularly consult with your tax professional to ensure compliance and take advantage of available tax-saving opportunities.

Conclusion

Understanding the tax implications of real estate investing is vital for optimizing your investment returns and maintaining compliance with tax laws. By taking advantage of deductions, understanding capital gains tax strategies, choosing the right entity structure, and engaging in proactive tax planning, you can minimize your tax liability and maximize the profitability of your real estate investments. Consult with tax professionals who specialize in real estate taxation to develop a tax strategy that aligns with your investment goals and ensures long-term success in real estate investing.

BUILDING A REAL ESTATE TEAM: BROKERS, CONTRACTORS, LAWYERS, AND ACCOUNTANTS

Building a strong and reliable real estate team is essential for success in the complex world of real estate investing. A team of experienced professionals can provide valuable expertise, guidance, and support throughout the investment process. In this chapter, we explore the key roles of brokers, contractors, lawyers, and accountants in real estate investing and how to build an effective team.

Real Estate Brokers

Real estate brokers play a crucial role in the buying and selling of properties. They are licensed professionals who assist investors in identifying investment opportunities, negotiating deals, and facilitating transactions. Here are some considerations when working with real estate brokers:

- Experience and Expertise: Look for brokers who specialize in the type of properties and markets you are interested in. Experienced brokers have in-depth knowledge of local market trends, property values, and investment opportunities.

- Market Insights: Brokers provide valuable market insights, including comparable sales data, rental rates, and demand-supply dynamics. Their expertise can help you make informed investment decisions and identify properties with strong potential.

- Access to Listings: Brokers have access to multiple listing services (MLS) and off-market properties. They can help you find properties that meet your investment criteria and have access to a broader range of opportunities than what is publicly available.

- Negotiation Skills: Brokers are skilled negotiators who can advocate for your interests and secure favorable purchase or sale terms. Their expertise can help you navigate complex negotiations and achieve the best possible outcomes.

- Networking and Connections: A reputable broker has a vast network of industry professionals, including contractors, lawyers, and lenders. This network can be valuable in connecting you with trusted professionals and expanding your real estate team.

Contractors and Construction Professionals

Contractors and construction professionals are essential when undertaking property renovations, repairs, or new construction projects. Selecting reliable contractors is crucial to ensure quality work, timely completion, and cost-effective solutions. Consider the following when working with contractors:

- Reputation and References: Research the reputation and track record of contractors before hiring them. Seek recommendations from other investors, check online reviews, and request references from past clients to ensure their reliability and competence.

- Experience and Specializations: Contractors with experience in real estate investing and knowledge of specific property types or renovation projects can provide valuable insights and cost-effective solutions. Choose contractors who specialize in the type of work you require.

- Licensing and Insurance: Ensure that contractors have the necessary licenses and insurance coverage, including liability and worker's compensation insurance. This protects you from potential liabilities and ensures that the work is performed by qualified professionals.

- Transparent Contracts and Timelines: Establish clear expectations, scope of work, timelines, and payment terms in written contracts. This helps prevent misunderstandings and ensures that the project progresses smoothly.

- Communication and Project Management: Effective communication is crucial for successful contractor relationships. Maintain regular communication, discuss project milestones, and address any issues or changes promptly. Contractors who are responsive and proactive in project management contribute to a smooth renovation or construction process.

Real Estate Lawyers

Real estate lawyers play a critical role in navigating the legal complexities of real estate transactions, contracts, and compliance. Working with a qualified real estate lawyer is essential to protect your interests and ensure legal compliance. Consider the following when engaging a real estate lawyer:

- Expertise in Real Estate Law: Choose a lawyer who specializes in real estate law and has a deep understanding of local, state, and federal regulations. Their expertise ensures that your transactions, contracts, and legal matters are handled correctly.

- Transaction Support: Real estate lawyers assist in reviewing and drafting purchase agreements, lease agreements, and other contracts related to real estate transactions. They ensure that the terms and conditions are favorable, protect your rights, and minimize potential risks.

- Title Search and Due Diligence: Real estate lawyers conduct title searches to ensure that the property you are purchasing has a clear title, free from any liens or encumbrances. They also perform due diligence to identify any legal issues or concerns associated with the property.

- Legal Advice and Guidance: Real estate lawyers provide legal advice on various matters, such as landlord-tenant disputes, property zoning and land use regulations, tax implications, and entity structuring. Their expertise helps you make informed decisions and navigate legal complexities.

- Closing and Escrow Services: Real estate lawyers oversee the closing process, ensuring that all legal documents are properly executed, funds are transferred securely, and the transaction is completed according to legal requirements.

- Litigation and Dispute Resolution: In the event of legal disputes or litigation related to your real estate investments, a real estate lawyer can represent your interests and guide you through the legal process.

Accountants and Tax Professionals

Accountants and tax professionals are instrumental in managing the financial aspects of your real estate investments and ensuring compliance with tax laws. Their expertise helps you optimize your tax strategy, maintain accurate financial records, and maximize your investment returns. Consider the following when working with accountants and tax professionals:

- Real Estate Tax Knowledge: Choose professionals who specialize in real estate taxation and have a thorough understanding of the tax implications specific to real estate investing. They can help you identify tax-saving opportunities, deductions, and credits that are applicable to your investments.

- Bookkeeping and Financial Statements: Accountants assist in maintaining accurate financial records, tracking income and expenses, and preparing financial statements. This ensures proper accounting practices, supports tax filings, and provides a clear overview of your investment performance.

- Tax Planning and Compliance: Accountants and tax professionals develop tax strategies tailored to your real estate investments. They help you navigate complex tax laws, comply with reporting requirements, and identify potential deductions and credits to minimize your tax liability.

- 1031 Exchanges and Capital Gains: Accountants can advise on 1031 exchanges, which allow you to defer capital gains taxes by reinvesting the proceeds from the sale of one property into a like-kind property. They ensure compliance with the specific rules and timelines associated with 1031 exchanges.

- Entity Structuring and Tax Optimization: Accountants provide guidance on choosing the most appropriate entity structure for your real estate investments, considering tax implications and liability protection. They help optimize your tax position by evaluating the pros and cons of different entity structures.

- Tax Filings and Compliance: Accountants handle the preparation and filing of tax returns for your real estate investments. They ensure accuracy, compliance with tax laws, and timely submission of required documents.

Building Your Real Estate Team

Building a real estate team involves finding professionals who align with your investment goals, values, and expectations. Here are some strategies to build an effective real estate team:

- Research and Referrals: Conduct thorough research and seek referrals from other investors, industry professionals, and local real estate associations. Look for professionals with experience in real estate investing and a strong track record.

- Interview and Evaluate: Interview potential team members to assess their expertise, communication style, responsiveness, and compatibility with your investment strategy. Ask for references and follow up on them to gather insights from their past clients.

- Collaboration and Communication: Building a successful team requires open and effective communication. Establish clear lines of communication and regular check-ins with your team members to ensure everyone is aligned, informed, and working towards common goals.

- Team Coordination: Encourage collaboration among team members by facilitating communication and coordination between them. This ensures that everyone is working together seamlessly and leveraging each other's expertise for the benefit of your real estate investments.

- Regular Evaluation and Feedback: Continuously evaluate the performance of your team members and provide constructive feedback. Regularly assess whether they are meeting your expectations and contributing to the success of your real estate endeavors. If needed, make adjustments to your team to ensure you have the right professionals supporting your investments.

- Professional Development and Continuous Learning: Encourage your team members to engage in professional development and stay updated on industry trends, regulations, and best practices. This ongoing learning ensures that your team members are equipped with the latest knowledge and can provide you with informed advice and guidance.

Remember that building a real estate team is not a one-time process but an ongoing endeavor. As your real estate portfolio grows, you may need to expand your team or make changes to adapt to new challenges and opportunities. Regularly assess your team's performance, seek feedback from your team members, and make adjustments as necessary to maintain a strong and reliable real estate team.

Conclusion

Building a strong and reliable real estate team is a crucial aspect of successful real estate investing. Brokers, contractors, lawyers, and accountants play essential roles in different stages of the investment process, providing expertise, guidance, and support. By carefully selecting experienced professionals, fostering effective communication and collaboration, and regularly evaluating your team's performance, you can build a team that supports your investment goals and contributes to your long-term success in real estate investing. Remember, a well-assembled real estate team is an invaluable asset that can help you navigate challenges, mitigate risks, and maximize the profitability of your real estate investments.

REAL ESTATE INVESTMENT TRUSTS (REITS): A DIFFERENT APPROACH

Real Estate Investment Trusts (REITs) offer a unique and accessible way for investors to participate in the real estate market without directly owning and managing properties. In this chapter, we explore the concept of REITs, their benefits and considerations, and how they provide investors with a different approach to real estate investing.

What are REITs?

A Real Estate Investment Trust (REIT) is a company that owns, operates, or finances income-generating real estate properties. REITs allow individual investors to pool their money and invest in a professionally managed portfolio of real estate assets. These assets can include various property types such as residential buildings, commercial properties, industrial facilities, healthcare facilities, and even infrastructure projects.

Benefits of Investing in REITs

Investing in REITs offers several advantages that make them an attractive investment option for individuals seeking exposure to the real estate market:

- Diversification: REITs provide investors with the opportunity to diversify their portfolios across different property types, locations, and markets. By investing in a REIT, you can gain exposure to a broad range of real estate assets that would be difficult to achieve through direct ownership.

- Accessibility: REITs are publicly traded entities listed on stock exchanges. This means that investors can easily buy and sell REIT shares, making them a highly liquid investment compared to owning individual properties. This accessibility allows investors to enter and exit the real estate market more readily.

- Professional Management: REITs are managed by experienced professionals who handle property acquisition, leasing, property management, and other operational aspects. Investors benefit from the expertise and industry knowledge of the REIT's management team, saving them from the day-to-day responsibilities of property ownership.

- Income Generation: REITs are required by law to distribute a significant portion of their taxable income to shareholders in the form of dividends. This distribution can provide a steady income stream to investors, making REITs an attractive option for those seeking regular cash flow.

- Potential for Capital Appreciation: REITs offer the potential for capital appreciation as the underlying real estate assets increase in value over time. Investors can benefit from the appreciation of the properties held within the REIT portfolio without directly owning them.

- Tax Efficiency: REITs are structured in a way that allows them to pass through the majority of their taxable income to shareholders. This results in the avoidance of double taxation at the corporate level, as the income is taxed only at the individual shareholder's level. This tax-efficient structure can enhance overall returns for investors.

- Transparency and Reporting: REITs are subject to stringent regulatory requirements, including regular financial reporting and transparency standards. This ensures that investors have access to reliable information about the REIT's financial health, performance, and underlying assets.

Considerations and Risks

While REITs offer several benefits, it is important for investors to consider the following aspects and risks associated with investing in REITs:

- Market and Economic Conditions: Like any investment, REITs are influenced by market and economic conditions. Factors such as changes in interest rates, supply and demand dynamics, and macroeconomic trends can impact the performance of REITs.

- Interest Rate Sensitivity: REITs can be sensitive to changes in interest rates. Rising interest rates can increase borrowing costs for REITs and potentially affect their profitability and valuations. It is important to assess the interest rate environment and its potential impact on REIT investments.

- Market and Sector Risk: Different property sectors within the REIT market may have varying levels of risk and performance. For example, a downturn in the commercial real estate sector can negatively impact commercial REITs. Investors should consider the specific sectors in which a REIT operates and evaluate their outlook and potential risks.

- Management Quality: The performance of a REIT is heavily influenced by the expertise and capabilities of its management team. Investors should assess the track record, experience, and reputation of the REIT's management team to ensure they have the necessary skills to navigate the real estate market effectively.

- Dividend Fluctuations: While REITs are known for their dividend distributions, the amount and consistency of dividends can vary. Investors should review the REIT's dividend history and dividend payout policies to understand the stability and potential for future income generation.

- Liquidity and Price Volatility: While REITs offer liquidity compared to direct property ownership, their shares can still experience price volatility in the stock market. Investors should be prepared for potential fluctuations in share prices and carefully consider their investment horizon and risk tolerance.

- Tax Considerations: While REITs offer tax advantages, investors should consult with tax professionals to understand the specific tax implications based on their individual circumstances. Tax rules can vary depending on the jurisdiction and investor's tax status.

Types of REITs

There are different types of REITs that investors can consider based on their investment objectives and preferences:

- Equity REITs: Equity REITs own and operate income-generating properties. They generate revenue from rental income and property appreciation. Equity REITs focus on acquiring, managing, and leasing properties across various sectors.

- Mortgage REITs: Mortgage REITs invest in real estate debt, such as mortgages and mortgage-backed securities. They earn income from the interest generated by the mortgage loans they hold. Mortgage REITs are more focused on the financing side of real estate investments.

- Hybrid REITs: Hybrid REITs combine elements of both equity and mortgage REITs. They invest in both properties and real estate debt instruments, offering a balanced approach to real estate investing.

- Specialty REITs: Specialty REITs focus on specific property sectors or niche areas within the real estate market, such as healthcare facilities, data centers, self-storage facilities, or timberlands. These REITs provide targeted exposure to specialized sectors.

Building a Portfolio with REITs

Incorporating REITs into a diversified investment portfolio can provide investors with exposure to the real estate market and potential diversification benefits. Here are some considerations when building a portfolio with REITs:

- Assess Investment Objectives: Determine your investment goals, risk tolerance, and desired exposure to the real estate market. This will help you decide on the allocation of your portfolio to REITs.

- Research and Select REITs: Conduct thorough research on different REITs, considering factors such as the quality of their real estate assets, management expertise, financial performance, and dividend history. Diversify your portfolio by selecting REITs across different sectors and geographies.

- Monitor Performance: Regularly review the performance of the REITs in your portfolio and stay informed about market and sector trends. Monitor changes in the REIT's fundamentals, dividend distributions, and market conditions to make informed investment decisions.

- Consider Risk Management: Incorporate risk management strategies by diversifying your REIT holdings, considering the economic cycle, and regularly rebalancing your portfolio to align with your investment objectives.

- Seek Professional Advice: If you are new to REIT investing or require guidance, consult with a financial advisor or investment professional who specializes in real estate investments. They can help you navigate the complexities of the REIT market and design a portfolio strategy that aligns with your investment goals and risk tolerance.

Conclusion

Real Estate Investment Trusts (REITs) provide investors with a unique approach to participate in the real estate market. With their potential for diversification, accessibility, professional management, income generation, and tax benefits, REITs offer an attractive investment option for individuals looking to gain exposure to real estate without the challenges of direct property ownership.

Investing in REITs requires careful consideration of factors such as market conditions, interest rate sensitivity, management quality, and specific risks associated with different sectors. It is important to conduct thorough research, evaluate the track record of REITs, and assess their fit within your investment portfolio.

By incorporating REITs into a diversified investment strategy, investors can benefit from potential capital appreciation, income generation, and diversification benefits. Regular monitoring and ongoing assessment of performance, along with prudent risk management, are essential for optimizing the potential of REIT investments.

As with any investment, it is recommended to seek advice from financial professionals who specialize in real estate investments and understand the intricacies of the REIT market. Their expertise can provide valuable guidance, help align your investment strategy with your goals, and navigate the complexities of investing in REITs.

Remember, REITs are a different approach to real estate investing, offering accessibility, diversification, and professional management. Incorporating them into a well-rounded investment portfolio can enhance overall returns, provide exposure to the real estate market, and potentially contribute to long-term investment success.

DIGITAL REAL ESTATE: EXPLORING THE WORLD OF ONLINE PROPERTIES

The digital era has brought about a new dimension of real estate investing—digital real estate. Just as physical properties can generate income and appreciate in value, online properties have emerged as valuable assets that offer unique investment opportunities. In this chapter, we delve into the world of digital real estate, exploring its various forms, investment potential, and considerations for investors.

Understanding Digital Real Estate

Digital real estate refers to virtual properties or assets that exist in the online world. These assets can take different forms and serve various purposes. Here are some key types of digital real estate:

- Domain Names: Domain names are the addresses of websites on the internet. Just as location is crucial in physical real estate, a domain name's value lies in its relevance, memorability, and potential for attracting online traffic. Valuable domain names can be sold or leased, providing income and potential capital appreciation.

- Websites: Websites are virtual properties that serve as online platforms for businesses, blogs, e-commerce, and various online activities. Well-designed and content-rich websites can attract visitors, generate revenue through advertising, affiliate marketing, or e-commerce sales, and be monetized through various strategies.

- E-Commerce Stores: E-commerce stores are online marketplaces where products or services are bought and sold. These virtual storefronts can be lucrative investments, leveraging the power of online shopping trends and consumer behavior. E-commerce stores can be built from scratch or acquired as existing businesses.

- Digital Products: Digital products include e-books, online courses, software applications, stock photos, music, and other digital assets that can be sold or licensed online. Investing in digital products involves creating or acquiring high-quality digital content that appeals to a specific target audience.

- Social Media Channels: Social media channels, such as popular accounts or pages on platforms like Instagram, YouTube, or TikTok, have become digital real estate assets. These channels can attract a large following, which can be leveraged for advertising partnerships, influencer marketing, or promoting products and services.

- Virtual Real Estate: Virtual worlds and online games have their own digital real estate market. In these virtual environments, users can own and develop virtual land, buildings, and properties. Virtual real estate can be monetized through virtual commerce, renting or selling virtual spaces, or offering virtual experiences.

Benefits of Investing in Digital Real Estate

Investing in digital real estate offers several benefits that make it an attractive option for investors looking to diversify their portfolios and tap into the online economy:

- Global Reach: Digital real estate provides access to a global audience. Online properties are not limited by physical boundaries, allowing investors to reach customers and clients worldwide, thereby expanding their potential market.

- Scalability and Flexibility: Digital properties have the potential for scalability, as they can be easily replicated or expanded without the constraints of physical space. They also offer flexibility in terms of management, operations, and scaling up or down based on market demand.

- Lower Barrier to Entry: Compared to traditional real estate investments, digital real estate often has a lower barrier to entry. Starting an online business or acquiring digital assets can require less upfront capital and ongoing expenses compared to physical properties.

- 24/7 Availability and Automation: Online properties operate around the clock, providing continuous income potential. Additionally, automation tools and online platforms allow for streamlined operations and scalability, reducing the need for extensive manual labor.

- Potential for Passive Income: Well-established digital properties can generate passive income through advertising, affiliate marketing, e-commerce sales, or licensing digital products. This passive income potential makes digital real estate an appealing option for those seeking income diversification.

- Emerging Market Potential: The digital landscape continues to evolve and expand, presenting new opportunities for innovation and growth. Investing in digital real estate allows investors to tap into emerging markets and trends, such as the rise of e-commerce, online education, digital content consumption, and virtual experiences.

Considerations for Digital Real Estate Investors

While investing in digital real estate offers unique advantages, it's essential to consider the following factors and best practices to make informed investment decisions:

- Market Research and Due Diligence: Thorough market research is crucial to identify niche markets, assess demand, and evaluate the potential profitability of digital real estate opportunities. Conduct due diligence on domain names, websites, e-commerce stores, or other digital assets before acquiring or investing.

- Quality and Content: Quality content and user experience are vital for digital properties to attract and retain visitors. Investing in digital real estate often requires creating or acquiring high-quality content that resonates with the target audience, ensuring that the property stands out in a competitive online landscape.

- Search Engine Optimization (SEO): Understanding and implementing effective SEO strategies can enhance the visibility and discoverability of digital properties. Optimizing websites, e-commerce stores, and digital content for search engines increases the likelihood of attracting organic traffic and potential customers.

- Monetization Strategies: Determine the most suitable monetization strategies for your digital real estate investments. This could include advertising, affiliate marketing, e-commerce sales, digital product sales, subscriptions, or partnerships. Explore multiple revenue streams to maximize income potential.

- Security and Data Protection: Cybersecurity and data protection are crucial considerations when investing in digital real estate. Implement robust security measures, use reputable hosting providers, and ensure compliance with privacy regulations to protect your investments and the personal information of users or customers.

- Digital Marketing and Promotion: Developing effective digital marketing strategies is essential to drive traffic, build brand awareness, and generate leads for your online properties. Explore social media marketing, content marketing, email marketing, influencer partnerships, and other digital marketing channels to reach your target audience.

- Stay Current with Technology and Trends: The digital landscape is constantly evolving, with emerging technologies and changing consumer behavior shaping the market. Stay updated with the latest trends, innovations, and best practices in digital marketing, e-commerce, and online user experiences to remain competitive and adapt to shifting market dynamics.

Conclusion

Digital real estate offers investors a unique avenue to tap into the online economy, diversify their portfolios, and leverage the global reach of the internet. Domain names, websites, e-commerce stores, digital products, social media channels, and virtual real estate are all forms of digital assets that hold value and income-generating potential.

Investing in digital real estate requires a deep understanding of the online landscape, thorough market research, and strategic decision-making. By focusing on quality content, effective monetization strategies, and staying attuned to evolving technologies and trends, investors can harness the benefits of digital real estate and capitalize on the opportunities presented by the digital era.

As with any investment, it is essential to conduct due diligence, seek professional advice when needed, and continuously monitor and optimize your digital real estate assets. With careful planning and a proactive approach, investing in digital real estate can be a rewarding venture that opens doors to the vast potential of the online world.

INTERNATIONAL REAL ESTATE: INVESTING BEYOND BORDERS

Investing in international real estate provides opportunities for diversification, potential for higher returns, and exposure to different markets and economies. In this chapter, we explore the world of international real estate investing, including its benefits, considerations, and strategies for success.

Benefits of International Real Estate Investing

Investing in international real estate offers several benefits that make it an attractive option for investors:

- Diversification: Investing in real estate assets outside of your home country allows for diversification, reducing risk by spreading investments across different markets. This diversification can help mitigate the impact of localized economic fluctuations or market downturns.

- Potential for Higher Returns: Certain international markets may offer higher growth potential and returns compared to domestic real estate markets. Investing in emerging economies or markets with high demand and limited supply can lead to significant capital appreciation and rental income.

- Access to Emerging Markets: International real estate investing provides access to emerging markets that are experiencing rapid economic growth and urban development. These markets often present untapped opportunities for investors looking to capitalize on expanding economies and rising property values.

- Currency Diversification: Investing in international real estate allows for exposure to different currencies. This can serve as a hedge against currency risks and provide potential currency appreciation benefits, especially when investing in countries with strengthening currencies.

- Lifestyle and Personal Use: International real estate investments can provide opportunities for personal enjoyment, such as vacation homes or retirement properties. Owning a property in a desirable location allows for personal use while potentially generating rental income when not in use.

Considerations for International Real Estate Investing

While international real estate investing offers unique advantages, it's crucial to consider the following factors and conduct thorough due diligence:

- Market Research and Local Knowledge: Research the target market extensively to understand its economic conditions, real estate trends, legal framework, and cultural factors. Local knowledge is essential for identifying market dynamics, growth potential, and potential challenges.

- Legal and Regulatory Considerations: Each country has its own legal and regulatory framework governing real estate investments. Familiarize yourself with the local laws, regulations, and procedures related to property ownership, taxes, and foreign investment restrictions.

- Political and Economic Stability: Evaluate the political stability and economic conditions of the target country. Political instability or economic downturns can significantly impact the real estate market and investment returns. Consider countries with a stable political environment and robust economic indicators.

- Local Partner or Expertise: Engaging a local partner, real estate agent, or consultant with expertise in the target market can provide invaluable guidance and insights. They can help navigate the local landscape, facilitate property transactions, and ensure compliance with local regulations.

- Currency Risks: Investing in international real estate exposes investors to currency risks. Fluctuations in exchange rates can impact the value of investments, rental income, and repatriation of funds. Consider currency hedging strategies or consult with financial professionals to manage currency risks.

- Tax Implications: Understand the tax implications of investing in foreign real estate, including taxes on rental income, capital gains, and inheritance taxes. Consult with tax advisors who specialize in international taxation to ensure compliance and optimize tax planning.

- Property Management and Maintenance: Consider the practical aspects of property management, especially if you are investing in a different country. Determine if you will manage the property yourself or engage local property management services to handle tenant relations, maintenance, and rental collection.

Strategies for International Real Estate Investing

To succeed in international real estate investing, consider the following strategies:

- Thorough Due Diligence: Conduct extensive research on the target market, including its economic indicators, real estate performance, supply and demand dynamics, and growth prospects.

- Location Selection: Identify locations with strong fundamentals, such as growing economies, stable political environments, and favorable demographics. Look for areas experiencing urban development, infrastructure improvements, and increased foreign investment.

- Partnerships and Networking: Establish relationships with local professionals, including real estate agents, attorneys, and property managers, who have expertise in the target market. They can provide valuable insights, access to off-market opportunities, and guidance throughout the investment process.

- Diversification: Consider diversifying your international real estate portfolio by investing in multiple countries or regions. This helps spread risk and allows you to capitalize on different market conditions and economic cycles.

- Asset Class Selection: Evaluate different types of real estate assets, such as residential properties, commercial buildings, retail spaces, or industrial warehouses, based on their potential for rental income, capital appreciation, and market demand in the target location.

- Risk Management: Conduct thorough risk assessments and develop risk management strategies. This includes understanding market risks, conducting property inspections, obtaining title insurance, and considering appropriate insurance coverage for international properties.

- Local Financing Options: Explore financing options available in the target country, such as local banks or financial institutions. Local financing can provide advantages, including access to competitive interest rates and a better understanding of the local lending landscape.

- Exit Strategy: Develop an exit strategy for your international real estate investments. Consider factors such as market conditions, investment horizon, potential capital gains taxes, and repatriation of funds. Having a clear exit plan allows you to maximize returns and navigate the process smoothly.

Conclusion

Investing in international real estate offers investors the opportunity for diversification, higher returns, and exposure to emerging markets. It is crucial to conduct thorough market research, understand local regulations, and mitigate risks associated with investing in foreign countries.

By carefully selecting target markets, partnering with local experts, and implementing effective risk management strategies, investors can navigate the complexities of international real estate investing and capitalize on the potential opportunities offered by global real estate markets.

International real estate investing requires a proactive approach, ongoing monitoring of market conditions, and adaptability to local regulations and cultural nuances. When executed with careful planning and due diligence, international real estate investments can be a rewarding addition to an investment portfolio, providing both financial returns and the potential for personal enjoyment of properties in desirable locations across the globe.

SUSTAINABILITY IN REAL ESTATE: INVESTING IN THE FUTURE

Sustainability has become a critical consideration in the real estate industry, as investors recognize the importance of environmentally conscious and socially responsible practices. In this chapter, we explore the concept of sustainability in real estate investing, its benefits, key strategies, and the role it plays in shaping the future of the industry.

Understanding Sustainability in Real Estate

Sustainability in real estate refers to the integration of environmentally friendly, socially responsible, and economically viable practices throughout the lifecycle of a property. It encompasses a wide range of factors, including energy efficiency, resource conservation, waste management, community engagement, and occupant well-being. Sustainable real estate aims to minimize negative environmental impacts, enhance social equity, and promote long-term economic viability.

Benefits of Sustainable Real Estate Investing

Investing in sustainable real estate offers several benefits for investors, communities, and the environment:

- Financial Performance: Sustainable properties have the potential for enhanced financial performance. They often attract high-quality tenants, command premium rental rates, and experience lower vacancy rates. Additionally, sustainable features can lead to operational cost savings through reduced energy consumption and maintenance expenses.

- Risk Mitigation: Sustainability practices can help mitigate risks associated with climate change, regulatory changes, and evolving consumer preferences. Investing in properties that meet or exceed sustainability standards reduces the exposure to physical and regulatory risks, ensuring long-term value preservation.

- Market Demand and Tenant Attraction: Sustainable properties appeal to an increasing number of tenants and occupiers who prioritize sustainability and environmental responsibility. By investing in sustainable real estate, investors can attract a broader tenant pool, reduce vacancy rates, and strengthen lease agreements.

- Enhanced Asset Value: Sustainable properties often experience increased asset value due to their attractiveness to investors, reduced operational costs, and the potential for future regulatory incentives. These properties are well-positioned for long-term value appreciation in an evolving market.

- Improved Indoor Environment: Sustainable buildings prioritize indoor environmental quality, leading to healthier and more productive spaces for occupants. Features such as efficient ventilation, natural lighting, and low-toxicity materials contribute to enhanced occupant comfort and well-being.

- Positive Environmental Impact: Sustainable real estate reduces carbon emissions, energy consumption, water usage, and waste generation. By investing in sustainable properties, investors contribute to environmental preservation and help address the global challenge of climate change.

Strategies for Sustainable Real Estate Investing

To integrate sustainability into real estate investments, consider the following strategies:

- Energy Efficiency and Renewable Energy: Incorporate energy-efficient features, such as efficient HVAC systems, insulation, LED lighting, and smart building technologies. Consider integrating renewable energy sources, such as solar panels or wind turbines, to reduce reliance on fossil fuels and lower carbon emissions.

- Green Building Certifications: Seek green building certifications, such as LEED (Leadership in Energy and Environmental Design) or BREEAM (Building Research Establishment Environmental Assessment Method), which provide third-party validation of a property's sustainability performance. These certifications demonstrate a commitment to sustainability and can enhance the marketability and value of the property.

- Water Conservation: Implement water-efficient fixtures, such as low-flow toilets and faucets, rainwater harvesting systems, and efficient irrigation methods for landscaping. By reducing water consumption, investors can minimize the strain on local water resources and potentially lower operating costs.

- Waste Management and Recycling: Develop waste management strategies that prioritize recycling, composting, and responsible waste disposal practices. Encourage tenants to participate in recycling programs and provide designated areas for waste separation within the property.

- Green Roofs and Sustainable Landscaping: Incorporate green roofs, rooftop gardens, or vegetative coverings to improve insulation, reduce urban heat island effect, and support biodiversity. Design sustainable landscapes that utilize native and drought-tolerant plants, promote water conservation, and minimize the need for chemical pesticides or fertilizers.

- Social Sustainability and Community Engagement: Consider the social impact of real estate investments by engaging with the local community. This can involve supporting local businesses, providing community spaces, promoting inclusivity and accessibility, and contributing to social initiatives that enhance the quality of life for residents.

- Lifecycle Assessment and Green Retrofitting: Assess the environmental impact of existing properties through lifecycle assessments. Identify opportunities for green retrofitting, such as energy-efficient upgrades, water-saving measures, and sustainable material choices, to improve the environmental performance of older buildings.

- Environmental, Social, and Governance (ESG) Integration: Incorporate environmental, social, and governance factors into the investment decision-making process. Evaluate the sustainability performance of potential investments, consider ESG risks and opportunities, and align investment strategies with sustainability goals.

- Engage with Sustainable Real Estate Networks and Associations: Join sustainable real estate networks and industry associations to stay informed about best practices, emerging trends, and technological advancements in sustainable real estate. Engaging with these networks can provide valuable insights and opportunities for collaboration.

The Role of Green Financing and Incentives

Green financing and incentives play a crucial role in promoting sustainable real estate investments. Governments, financial institutions, and organizations offer various programs that support sustainable initiatives, including:

- Green Loans and Mortgages: Financial institutions provide loans and mortgages with favorable terms for properties that meet specific sustainability criteria. These loans often offer lower interest rates, longer repayment periods, or flexible financing options.

- Energy Efficiency Grants and Rebates: Governments and utility companies offer grants and rebates to support energy-efficient upgrades and renewable energy installations. These incentives can offset the upfront costs of implementing sustainable features and improve the financial feasibility of sustainable projects.

- Tax Benefits: Some jurisdictions provide tax incentives, such as tax credits or deductions, for sustainable real estate investments. These incentives can include tax breaks for energy-efficient improvements, renewable energy installations, or green building certifications.

- Green Bonds: Green bonds are investment instruments that raise capital specifically for environmentally friendly projects. Investing in green bonds can provide investors with financial returns while supporting sustainable real estate initiatives.

Conclusion

Sustainability in real estate investing has evolved from a niche consideration to a fundamental aspect of responsible investment practices. By incorporating sustainability principles into real estate investments, investors can achieve financial returns while contributing to environmental preservation, social well-being, and long-term value creation.

Investing in sustainable real estate offers benefits such as enhanced financial performance, risk mitigation, market demand, improved asset value, occupant well-being, and positive environmental impact. Strategies for sustainable real estate investing include energy efficiency, green building certifications, water conservation, waste management, social sustainability, and engagement with sustainable real estate networks.

Furthermore, green financing and incentives play a crucial role in promoting sustainable practices and supporting sustainable real estate investments. These initiatives provide financial advantages, reduce barriers to entry, and incentivize the adoption of sustainable strategies.

As sustainability continues to gain prominence in the real estate industry, investors have the opportunity to shape the future by integrating sustainable practices into their investment strategies. By investing in sustainable real estate, investors contribute to a more resilient, environmentally responsible, and socially inclusive built environment that benefits both present and future generations.

CASE STUDIES: LESSONS FROM SUCCESSFUL REAL ESTATE INVESTORS

Real estate investing has proven to be a wealth-building strategy for many successful investors. In this chapter, we examine case studies of notable real estate investors, their strategies, and the lessons we can learn from their success. By analyzing these real-life examples, we can gain valuable insights and apply them to our own investment endeavors.

Case Study 1: Donald Bren- Mastering Land Development

Donald Bren, the chairman of Irvine Company, is renowned for his success in land development. His strategic acquisitions and development projects have transformed large tracts of land into thriving communities and commercial centers. Key lessons from Donald Bren's success include:

- Location is Key: Bren focused on acquiring land in prime locations with strong growth potential. Investing in well-located properties ensures long-term demand and appreciation.

- Long-Term Vision: Bren adopted a long-term perspective, patiently developing properties over time and anticipating future market trends. Real estate investing requires foresight and a commitment to the long-term success of projects.

- Value Creation: Bren added value through thoughtful planning, incorporating amenities, open spaces, and community infrastructure into his developments. By creating attractive and functional spaces, he maximized property value and appeal.

Case Study 2: Sam Zell- Contrarian Investing

Sam Zell, known as the "Grave Dancer," is a renowned contrarian investor who has successfully capitalized on distressed real estate opportunities. Key lessons from Sam Zell's success include:

- Timing is Crucial: Zell has a knack for identifying market cycles and investing during downturns. Being contrarian and buying when others are selling can lead to significant gains when markets recover.

- Risk Assessment: Zell carefully assesses the risks and potential rewards of distressed properties. Thorough due diligence and a deep understanding of the underlying value of the assets are critical for successful contrarian investing.

- Hands-On Management: Zell is actively involved in managing his investments and making strategic decisions. Hands-on management ensures that the right actions are taken to turn around distressed properties and maximize returns.

Case Study 3: Barbara Corcoran - Branding and Marketing

Barbara Corcoran, the founder of The Corcoran Group, achieved remarkable success through her branding and marketing strategies in the real estate industry. Key lessons from Barbara Corcoran's success include:

- Building a Strong Brand: Corcoran built a recognizable and trusted brand in the competitive real estate market. Developing a unique brand identity and delivering exceptional customer service can set investors apart from the competition.

- Effective Marketing: Corcoran utilized creative marketing tactics to generate buzz and attract buyers. Effective marketing strategies, such as leveraging media exposure and utilizing innovative advertising campaigns, can help investors reach a wider audience and generate interest in their properties.

- Building Relationships: Corcoran prioritized building strong relationships with clients and industry professionals. Networking, nurturing client relationships, and cultivating a strong referral network are essential for long-term success in real estate investing.

Case Study 4: Grant Cardone- Multi-Family Real Estate Investing

Grant Cardone, a successful entrepreneur and real estate investor, has achieved significant wealth through multi-family real estate investments. Key lessons from Grant Cardone's success include:

- Scale and Portfolio Growth: Cardone emphasizes the importance of scaling investments and building a large portfolio of cash-flowing properties. Diversifying across multiple properties and markets can mitigate risk and maximize cash flow potential.

- Market Research and Analysis: Cardone conducts thorough market research to identify markets with strong demand for rental properties. Investing in areas with population growth, job opportunities, and positive economic indicators increases the likelihood of stable rental income and property appreciation. Strategic Financing: Cardone leverages financing options, such as commercial loans, to acquire larger multi-family properties. Using other people's money and employing creative financing strategies can enable investors to scale their investments and maximize returns.

- Value-Add Strategies: Cardone implements value-add strategies, such as property renovations and improvements, to increase rental income and property value. By identifying properties with untapped potential and implementing strategic upgrades, investors can enhance cash flow and equity growth.

Case Study 5: Warren Buffett - Long-Term Investing

Warren Buffett, one of the most successful investors in history, has made strategic real estate investments as part of his overall investment approach. Key lessons from Warren Buffett's success include:

- Long-Term Mindset: Buffett emphasizes the importance of a long-term investment horizon. Real estate investing, like other asset classes, benefits from a patient approach that allows for value appreciation and the compounding effect of time.

- Value Investing: Buffett looks for undervalued properties or distressed assets that offer substantial potential for long-term value creation. By focusing on the underlying value of the property, investors can capitalize on opportunities that others may overlook.

- Cash Flow and Income: Buffett emphasizes the importance of generating consistent cash flow and income from real estate investments. Properties that generate regular rental income can provide a steady stream of cash flow and support long-term wealth creation.

- Risk Management: Buffett is known for his focus on risk management and preserving capital. Conducting thorough due diligence, assessing potential risks, and taking calculated investment decisions are key to successful real estate investing.

Conclusion

Case studies of successful real estate investors provide valuable insights and lessons that can be applied to our own investment strategies. From mastering land development and contrarian investing to branding and marketing, multi-family investing, and long-term value creation, these case studies illustrate the diverse approaches and strategies employed by successful investors.

Key takeaways include the importance of location, timing, risk assessment, hands-on management, branding, marketing, scale, market research, strategic financing, value-add strategies, a long-term mindset, cash flow generation, and effective risk management.

By studying and learning from the experiences of successful real estate investors, we can gain valuable knowledge and apply it to our own investment decisions.

Remember that while these case studies provide insights, each investment opportunity is unique, and it is crucial to conduct thorough research, exercise due diligence, and adapt strategies to specific market conditions and individual goals.

FUTURE OF REAL ESTATE INVESTING: TRENDS TO WATCH

The real estate industry is evolving rapidly, driven by technological advancements, changing demographics, and shifting market dynamics. To succeed in real estate investing, it is crucial to stay informed about emerging trends and adapt to the evolving landscape. In this chapter, we explore the future of real estate investing and highlight key trends that investors should watch.

Technology and Innovation

Technology continues to reshape the real estate industry, providing new opportunities and changing the way properties are developed, managed, and transacted. Key technological trends to watch include:

- Smart Buildings and IoT: The Internet of Things (IoT) enables connectivity and automation in buildings, allowing for energy efficiency, remote monitoring, predictive maintenance, and enhanced occupant experiences.

- Proptech Solutions: Proptech companies are leveraging technology to streamline property management, improve tenant experiences, enhance property valuation and due diligence, and facilitate online transactions and crowdfunding.
- Virtual Reality (VR) and Augmented Reality (AR): VR and AR technologies offer immersive experiences for property viewing, design visualization, and remote collaboration, eliminating geographical barriers and improving decision-making processes.
- Big Data and Analytics: Data analytics tools allow for better market insights, predictive modeling, risk assessment, and performance optimization in real estate investments.

Sustainability and ESG Investing

Sustainability and Environmental, Social, and Governance (ESG) considerations are gaining prominence in the real estate industry. Investors are increasingly focused on properties that promote energy efficiency, green building certifications, social responsibility, and community engagement. Key trends in sustainability and ESG investing include:

- Green Building Standards: Green building certifications, such as LEED and BREEAM, are becoming standard requirements for new developments and renovations, ensuring environmental performance and occupant well-being.

- Impact Investing: Investors are seeking opportunities that align with their values, investing in projects with positive social and environmental impacts, such as affordable housing, renewable energy installations, and sustainable urban development.
- ESG Integration: Environmental, social, and governance factors are being integrated into investment decision-making processes, ensuring responsible investment practices, risk mitigation, and long-term value creation.

Urbanization and Mixed-Use Developments

The ongoing global trend of urbanization is shaping the future of real estate investing. Urban areas are experiencing population growth, increased demand for mixed-use developments, and the transformation of cities into live-work-play environments. Key trends in urbanization and mixed-use developments include:

- Walkable Communities: Investors are focusing on properties in walkable neighborhoods that offer convenience, access to amenities, and a sense of community. Walkability is a key factor for attracting tenants and supporting property value appreciation.

- Live-Work-Play Environments: Mixed-use developments that combine residential, commercial, retail, and entertainment spaces are in high demand. These developments provide convenience, reduce commute times, and offer a vibrant lifestyle for residents.
- Adaptive Reuse: Adaptive reuse of underutilized properties, such as converting old factories into loft apartments or repurposing historic buildings for commercial use, presents opportunities for creative investments and revitalization of urban areas.

Demographic Shifts and Lifestyle Preferences

Changing demographics and lifestyle preferences are influencing real estate investment trends. Investors need to consider the following:

- Millennial and Gen Z Preferences: Younger generations prioritize experiences, sustainability, and flexibility. Real estate investments that cater to their preferences, such as co-living spaces, flexible workspaces, and smart homes, have strong potential for growth.
- Active Adult Communities: As the population ages, there is a growing demand for active adult

communities that provide amenities, healthcare services, and social engagement opportunities for retirees.

- Rise of Remote Work: The pandemic accelerated the adoption of remote work, leading to increased demand for suburban and rural properties that offer larger living spaces, home offices, and access to nature.

Real Estate Crowdfunding and Tokenization

Crowdfunding platforms and blockchain technology are revolutionizing real estate investing, making it more accessible and efficient. Key trends in real estate crowdfunding and tokenization include:

- Fractional Ownership: Investors can participate in real estate investments with lower capital requirements through fractional ownership platforms, allowing for diversification and reduced entry barriers.
- Tokenization: Blockchain technology enables the tokenization of real estate assets, creating digital tokens that represent fractional ownership. This increases liquidity, facilitates seamless transactions, and opens up global investment opportunities.

Changing Retail Landscape

The retail sector is undergoing significant transformation, driven by e-commerce, changing consumer behaviors, and the need for experiential retail spaces. Key trends in the retail landscape include:

- Omni-channel Retail: Retailers are adopting omni-channel strategies, integrating online and offline experiences to meet consumer demands. Investors should consider properties that can adapt to the evolving retail landscape and accommodate e-commerce fulfillment needs.
- Experiential Retail: Physical retail spaces are shifting towards experiential offerings, such as entertainment, dining, and interactive experiences. Investing in properties that provide unique and engaging experiences can attract tenants and drive foot traffic.

Co-living and Shared Spaces

The rise of co-living and shared spaces is changing the residential real estate landscape. Key trends in co-living and shared spaces include:

- Co-living Spaces: Co-living properties offer shared living spaces and amenities, catering to the needs of young professionals, students, and digital nomads. This trend provides affordable housing options and fosters a sense of community.
- Shared Workspaces: The popularity of shared workspaces, such as coworking spaces, is on the rise. Investors can explore opportunities in properties that accommodate the flexible working needs of freelancers, startups, and remote workers.

Conclusion

The future of real estate investing is shaped by technological advancements, sustainability considerations, urbanization, changing demographics, and evolving market trends. Investors who stay informed about these trends and adapt their strategies accordingly have the potential to capitalize on emerging opportunities and navigate the evolving real estate landscape successfully.

Key trends to watch include technology and innovation, sustainability and ESG investing, urbanization and mixed-use developments, demographic shifts and lifestyle preferences, real estate crowdfunding and tokenization, the changing retail landscape, and the growth of co-living and shared spaces.

As an investor, it is crucial to continuously educate yourself, conduct thorough market research, and stay attuned to evolving trends to make informed investment decisions. By embracing the future of real estate investing and being proactive in adapting to market dynamics, you can position yourself for long-term success and capitalize on the opportunities that lie ahead.

CREATING YOUR REAL ESTATE INVESTMENT PLAN: THE ROAD TO FINANCIAL FREEDOM

Building a successful real estate investment portfolio requires careful planning, strategic decision-making, and a well-defined investment plan. In this chapter, we will guide you through the process of creating your real estate investment plan, setting financial goals, assessing risk tolerance, identifying investment strategies, and executing your plan effectively.

Define Your Financial Goals

Start by clarifying your financial goals and aspirations. Ask yourself what you want to achieve through real estate investing. Your goals may include:

- Building Long-Term Wealth: Accumulating assets and generating passive income to achieve financial security and independence.
- Portfolio Diversification: Expanding your investment portfolio to mitigate risk and achieve a balanced asset allocation.

- Retirement Planning: Creating a stable income stream for retirement and ensuring financial comfort in your golden years.
- Funding Education: Investing in real estate to provide financial resources for your children's education.
- Achieving Financial Freedom: Replacing your current income and achieving the freedom to pursue your passions and lifestyle of choice.

By clearly defining your financial goals, you can align your investment strategy and make informed decisions to work towards achieving them.

Assess Your Risk Tolerance

Understanding your risk tolerance is essential in shaping your investment plan. Real estate investing involves various risks, including market fluctuations, tenant vacancies, property maintenance, and financing risks. Consider your risk tolerance by evaluating:

- Financial Stability: Assess your financial situation, including your income stability, existing debt, and emergency funds. Ensure you have a solid financial foundation before taking on higher-risk investments.

- Time Horizon: Determine your investment time horizon, considering factors such as your age, retirement plans, and the duration you are willing to hold your real estate investments. Longer time horizons may allow for higher-risk strategies.
- Emotional Resilience: Assess your ability to handle market volatility and stressful situations that may arise in real estate investing. Evaluate your emotional response to financial setbacks and fluctuations in property values.

By understanding your risk tolerance, you can select investment strategies and properties that align with your comfort level and overall financial objectives.

Choose Your Investment Strategies

Identify the investment strategies that align with your goals and risk tolerance. Common real estate investment strategies include:

- Buy and Hold: Acquiring properties with the intention of holding them for an extended period to generate rental income and long-term appreciation.

- Fix and Flip: Purchasing distressed properties, renovating them, and selling them quickly for a profit.
- Wholesaling: Facilitating the purchase and sale of properties without taking ownership, typically by assigning contracts to other investors.
- Real Estate Investment Trusts (REITs): Investing in publicly traded companies that own and manage income-generating real estate properties.
- Real Estate Syndication: Pooling funds with other investors to invest in larger, more lucrative real estate projects.
- Rental Property Investment: Acquiring residential or commercial properties to rent out and generate ongoing rental income.

Evaluate each strategy's advantages, disadvantages, and compatibility with your financial goals, risk tolerance, and available resources.

Conduct Market Research

Thorough market research is crucial for successful real estate investing. Key aspects of market research include:

- Location Analysis: Assess the economic growth, population trends, employment opportunities, infrastructure development, and desirability of potential investment locations.
- Property Demand: Understand the demand and supply dynamics for different types of properties in the target market. Analyze vacancy rates, rental rates, and property appreciation trends.
- Local Regulations: Familiarize yourself with local regulations, zoning laws, rental restrictions, and licensing requirements that may impact your investment.

Market research provides valuable insights to identify potential investment opportunities and make informed decisions. It helps you identify markets with strong growth potential, high rental demand, and favorable investment conditions.

- Property Analysis: Evaluate individual properties based on their financial performance, potential rental income, cash flow projections, and appreciation potential. Consider factors such as property condition, location, amenities, and market comparables.

By conducting thorough market research, you can identify promising investment opportunities and make informed decisions that align with your investment plan.

Develop a Financial Plan

Once you have identified your investment strategies and assessed potential opportunities, it's time to develop a comprehensive financial plan. Consider the following elements:

- Budgeting and Financing: Determine your investment budget and explore financing options such as traditional mortgages, private loans, partnerships, or creative financing strategies. Develop a plan for managing expenses, including property acquisition costs, renovations, property management fees, and ongoing maintenance.

- Cash Flow Analysis: Evaluate the potential cash flow of each investment property by estimating rental income and deducting expenses such as mortgage payments, property taxes, insurance, and property management fees. Ensure that the cash flow generated meets your financial goals and provides a sustainable income stream.

- Return on Investment (ROI): Calculate the projected ROI for each investment by considering factors such as rental income, property appreciation, tax benefits, and expenses. Assess the expected return relative to the level of risk involved.

- Exit Strategy: Develop a clear exit strategy for each investment. Determine when and how you plan to sell or exit a property, taking into account factors such as market conditions, capital gains taxes, and potential reinvestment opportunities.

A well-developed financial plan provides a roadmap for achieving your financial goals and helps you make informed investment decisions.

Implement and Monitor Your Plan

Once your investment plan is in place, it's time to start executing it. Take the following steps to implement your plan effectively:

- Property Acquisition: Execute property acquisitions based on your defined investment criteria and market research. Conduct due diligence, negotiate favorable terms, and ensure proper documentation and legal processes.

- Property Management: If you choose to manage your properties yourself, establish efficient property management processes. Alternatively, consider hiring a professional property management company to handle tenant screening, rent collection, maintenance, and other property-related tasks.

- Risk Management: Implement risk management strategies such as property insurance, contingency funds, and regular property inspections. Monitor market conditions and make adjustments to your portfolio as needed.

- Performance Monitoring: Regularly review the financial performance of your investments. Analyze cash flow, rental income, expenses, and overall returns. Adjust your strategies if needed to optimize performance and achieve your financial goals.

Continual Learning and Adaptation

Real estate investing is a dynamic field, and it's essential to stay updated with industry trends, market changes, and evolving regulations. Continual learning and adaptation are crucial for long-term success. Stay engaged by:

- Industry Education: Attend seminars, workshops, webinars, and conferences to enhance your knowledge of real estate investing. Join industry associations and networks to stay connected with fellow investors and professionals.

- Market Monitoring: Stay informed about market conditions, trends, and emerging opportunities. Keep track of rental rates, property values, economic indicators, and regulatory changes that may impact your investments.

- Network Building: Cultivate relationships with real estate professionals, fellow investors, and industry experts. Networking provides valuable insights, access to off-market deals, and potential partnerships for future investment opportunities.

By continually learning and adapting, you can optimize your investment strategies, identify new opportunities, and navigate the evolving real estate landscape effectively.

Conclusion

Creating a real estate investment plan is a crucial step on your journey to financial freedom. By defining your financial goals, assessing your risk tolerance, selecting investment strategies, conducting market research, developing a financial plan, implementing and monitoring your investments, and continually learning and adapting, you set yourself on the road to financial freedom through real estate investing.

Remember to regularly review and adjust your investment plan as needed to align with changing market conditions, personal circumstances, and financial goals. Real estate investing requires patience, diligence, and a long-term perspective. It is essential to stay disciplined, manage risks effectively, and make informed decisions based on thorough analysis and research.

Throughout your real estate investment journey, seek guidance from experienced professionals, consult with financial advisors, and learn from the successes and failures of other investors. Building a strong network and surrounding yourself with knowledgeable individuals can provide valuable insights, support, and opportunities for collaboration.

Lastly, remain focused on your long-term financial goals and stay committed to the plan you have developed. Real estate investing is a journey that requires dedication, perseverance, and a proactive approach. With careful planning and execution, real estate can be a powerful vehicle for building wealth, generating passive income, and ultimately achieving the financial freedom you desire.

Embrace the journey, stay adaptable, and continue to educate yourself as you navigate the exciting world of real estate investing. With a well-crafted investment plan, diligence, and a commitment to ongoing learning, you can unlock the potential for significant financial rewards and embark on the path to a more secure and prosperous future.

GLOSSARY OF TERMS

Amortization: This is the process of spreading out a loan into a series of fixed payments over time. The loan is fully paid off at the end of the amortization period, which typically spans several years.

Broker: A person licensed to represent home buyers or sellers for a commission. They assist in negotiation and transaction of real estate deals.

Closing Costs: These are the expenses, over and above the property price, that buyers and sellers normally incur to complete a real estate transaction.

Depreciation: In real estate, depreciation is a deduction that allows an investor to recover the cost of an income-producing property through yearly tax deductions.

Equity: This is the difference between the fair market value of the property and the amount still owed on its mortgage.

Foreclosure: This is the legal process by which a lender takes control of a property, evicts the homeowner, and sells the home after a homeowner is unable to make full principal and interest payments on his or her mortgage.

Gross Rent Multiplier (GRM): This is a ratio used in real estate to estimate the value of income-producing properties. It's calculated by dividing the property's price by its gross annual rental income.

Home Inspection: This is an examination of a real estate property's condition, usually performed in connection with the property's sale.

Interest Rate: This is the amount charged, expressed as a percentage of principal, by a lender to a borrower for the use of assets.

Joint Venture: This is a business arrangement in which two or more parties agree to pool their resources for the purpose of accomplishing a specific task, such as a real estate project.

Knockout Clause: A provision in a purchase contract that allows a seller to continue marketing the property to other buyers so that if a better offer is received, the original purchaser has a chance to match it.

Lien: This is a claim or legal right against assets that are used to secure a debt and that must be paid when the property is sold.

Multiple Listing Service (MLS): This is a service used by a group of real estate brokers. They band together to create an MLS that allows each of them to list each other's properties.

Net Operating Income (NOI): This is a calculation used to analyze the profitability of income-generating real estate investments. NOI equals all revenue from the property, minus all reasonably necessary operating expenses.

Open House: A scheduled period of time in which a house or other dwelling is designated to be open for viewing for potential buyers.

Principal: This is the amount of money that you originally agree to pay back on a loan, not including interest.

Quitclaim Deed: A legal instrument used to transfer interest in real property. The entity transferring its interest is called the grantor, and when the quitclaim deed is properly completed and executed, it transfers any interest the grantor has in the property to a recipient, called the grantee.

Real Estate Investment Trust (REIT): A REIT is a company that owns, operates or finances income-producing real estate.

Survey: A drawing or map showing the precise legal boundaries of a property, the location of improvements, easements, rights of way, encroachments, and other physical features.

Title: This is a document that gives evidence of an individual's ownership of property.

Underwriting: This is the process used by lenders to determine a borrower's creditworthiness. The underwriter assesses the risk of lending money to the borrower and establishes the terms of the loan.

Vacancy Rate: This is the percentage of all available units or space in a rental property that are vacant or unoccupied at a particular time.

Warranty Deed: This is a type of deed where the seller guarantees that he or she holds clear title to a piece of real estate and has a right to sell it to the buyer.

X-Factor: While not a standard real estate term, in the context of real estate investment, an 'X-factor' could refer to a unique or outstanding feature of a property that makes it particularly attractive to potential buyers or renters.

Yield: In real estate, yield refers to the annual net income that an investor receives, expressed as a percentage of the property's cost or market value. It's a measure of the profitability of an investment.

Zoning: Zoning refers to municipal or local laws or regulations that dictate how real property can and cannot be used in certain geographic areas. Zoning regulations can limit commercial or industrial use of land to prevent conflicts between landowners and protect the interests of a community.

www.ingramcontent.com/pod-product-compliance
Lightning Source LLC
Chambersburg PA
CBHW070635220526
45466CB00001B/179